My love must wait

You know his genius and
what gigantic strides he takes
in everything.   *Thomason*

If God has work for me to do
I cannot die.   *Martyn*

Inter-Varsity Press

My love must wait
The story of Henry Martyn

David Bentley-Taylor

INTER-VARSITY PRESS

Universities and Colleges Christian Fellowship,
39 Bedford Square, London WC1B 3EY

© INTER-VARSITY PRESS, LONDON

First edition September 1975

ISBN 0 85110 383 9

Printed in Great Britain by
Richard Clay (The Chaucer Press), Ltd.,
Bungay, Suffolk

Contents

1 The raw material

There was trouble in Cornwall one August morning in
1789, just as the French Revolution was breaking over
Europe. Out of the villages and lanes of the south-west,
where England begins to taper off into two blunt head-
lands, men were converging on the picturesque country
town of Truro beside the River Fal. On one side it was
soldiers, on the other tin miners, who came to block the
narrow streets with their noisy protest marches, demand-
ing wage increases without which, they declared, they
could not live.

And that very morning, among the crowded traffic of
pedestrians, pack-animals, horses and carts making their
way along the unsurfaced roads which criss-crossed the
rolling hills, a heavy, long-distance coach came right up
to the outskirts of Truro. Inside was John Wesley, in his
eighty-sixth year still fit enough for his work as evangelist
to the English people. There was no way through the
crowds to the chapel where he was due to preach, so the
coachman drove round by side-streets till he halted outside a building known as the Coinage Hall. And there
Wesley addressed twice as many people as could have got
into the chapel.

But that was nothing compared to his audience a few
days later at the Pit, beyond Truro by the village of
Gwennap, a kind of amphitheatre where grass had grown
over disused mine workings. Seventeen times in twenty-
seven years he had stood in the Pit and he surveyed the

scene once more with unconcealed delight. Almost thirty thousand people were present. It was normally like that at Gwennap. Those seventeen Sunday meetings were the biggest gatherings he faced anywhere in England. Wesley regarded it as the most magnificent spectacle to be seen this side of heaven. But that day he knew it was the end: 'I preached in the evening at the amphitheatre, I suppose for the last time, for my voice cannot now command the still-increasing multitude.'

It was at Gwennap that John Martyn, father of Henry Martyn, was born. Although so far from the great cities of London and Bristol, western Cornwall had witnessed remarkable industrial development, thanks to its mineral resources, which had been exploited since the dawn of history. Early in the eighteenth century a young engineer named William Lemon had made himself famous and wealthy by introducing a steam pumping-engine at a mine at St Hilary, near Penzance. Then he turned to Gwennap and commenced copper-mining on a large scale, using many of these engines.

As a result Gwennap became for almost a century the richest copper-mining district in the world and Lemon the foremost man in Cornwall, dominating Truro for thirty years till his death in 1760. His business was then taken over by his secretary, Thomas Daniell, described as 'a general merchant, tin smelter, and adventurer in mines on the largest scale'. John Martyn was for some years his chief clerk. He also served as accountant and cashier to his son, Ralph Allen Daniell, who became mayor of Truro, High Sheriff for Cornwall, and for seven years a Member of Parliament. Associated with these distinguished families, John Martyn's working life was devoted to a very successful industrial enterprise. He himself had a financial interest in the Wheal Unity Mine, but there seems no foundation for the suggestion that he ever went underground himself.

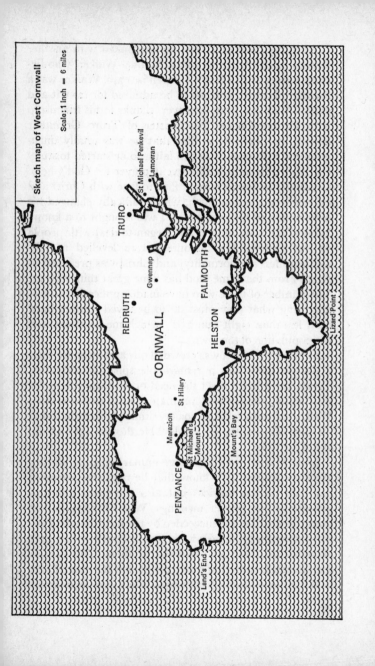

Sketch map of West Cornwall

Scale: 1 inch = 6 miles

St Michael Penkevil
Lamorran
TRURO
Gwennap
FALMOUTH
REDRUTH
CORNWALL
HELSTON
St Hilary
Marazion
St Michael's Mount
PENZANCE
Mount's Bay
Land's End
Lizard Point

At quite a different level he was linked with another famous Truro figure, the Rev. Samuel Walker, who became curate at St Mary's Church in 1746. Walker was a lover of pleasure, anxious to be admired for his wit and gaiety. Within a year, however, thanks to his friendship with George Conon, headmaster of Truro Grammar School, he began to realize that he was totally unacquainted with true Christian faith, so he started to study the Bible diligently, with fervent prayer for God's help. Gradually he found himself face to face with Christ and experienced the new birth, which radically changed his behaviour and his preaching. 'I was brought to a knowledge of the ways of God and began to deal with people as lost sinners. My discourses were levelled at self-righteousness and formality, and Christ was preached to them. From that time God has done great things for us. The number of those who have made application to me, enquiring what they must do to be saved, cannot have been less than eight hundred' (which meant about half the population of the town).

St Mary's Church was crowded out and for more than a decade there was a remarkable spiritual revival in Truro. In order to meet the need of so many people for instruction, prayer and intimate Christian fellowship, Walker started a religious society similar to those initiated all over the country by Wesley. He died in 1761 at the age of forty-six.

John Martyn was a young, unmarried man during Walker's lifetime. We know that he regularly attended not only church services but also the more informal gatherings and prayer meetings. When Walker passed from the scene he was succeeded by the Rev. Charles Pye, who strenuously opposed his predecessor's views and alienated all those who had shared them. This caused such dissatisfaction that many people left the church and held their own meetings elsewhere. They were nicknamed

'Walkerites', and met with much opposition as the originators of a schism from the established church. Since we know that after Walker's death John Martyn preferred the prayer meetings to the church, it would seem that he shared in both the dissatisfaction and the evangelical faith which lay behind it.

He married and had a son, also called John. Then his wife died. Later he married a girl named Fleming from Ilfracombe in Devon. They had many children, most of whom inherited the mother's weak constitution and died in infancy. Only the last three survived: Laura, born in 1779; Henry, born 18 February, 1781; and Sally, born in 1782, in which year their mother died. By that time John was sixteen. Their father never remarried and it is not known how he managed to carry on with his job and yet care for his little family. He lived right opposite the Coinage Hall, where Wesley preached. Henry Martyn was only eight years old at the time and he never mentions seeing or hearing Wesley, yet his life can be regarded as an outcome of Wesley's prodigious efforts to bring the gospel to the people of Cornwall over so many years.

Henry entered Truro Grammar School in 1788, when Dr Cornelius Cardew was the headmaster. He was described as 'a good-humoured, plain, little fellow, not particularly studious'. Although lively and cheerful, and encouraged to do well by his father, he passed through a stage of comparative idleness, trusting to his wits and not bothering to prepare his work properly. But Dr Cardew gave him a good grounding in Latin and Greek and he became an increasingly bright student. Being small and sensitive he was bullied by other boys, so Cardew put him in the charge of a senior boy named Kempthorne, son of an admiral from Helston, who acted as his protector and became one of the formative influences in Henry's early life.

Dr Cardew, Henry's father and his father's friends

were soon so impressed by his progress that they encouraged him to try for a scholarship to Oxford University. There was a link between the Grammar School and Exeter College, Oxford, so at the age of fifteen Henry travelled there alone by coach. However, someone else got the scholarship and in retrospect Henry was glad he had not stayed in Oxford, as the friends he made there were so debauched. Though his father still kept before him the goal of University education, Henry remained in Truro during the opening years of England's long war with France, which was to continue throughout the whole of his life.

Kempthorne, meanwhile, had gone to Cambridge University and greatly distinguished himself in mathematics. In the end, Henry followed him, entering St John's College in October 1797, when he was still only sixteen. At first his tutor was a little perplexed. He found Henry a quiet youth who had some knowledge of the classics but was lamentably deficient in mathematics, the subject he had to study. The tutor asked Shepherd, a second-year student, to try to help the boy, but he was not immediately successful. 'In sheer despair,' Shepherd recalled, 'Henry was about to go to the coach office and return next day to Truro. I urged him not to be so precipitate but to come to me again and have another try. After some time light suddenly seemed to flash upon his mind and he threw up his cap for joy.'

Henry did extremely well after that, partly from a desire to please his father: 'in truth his progress was so rapid that he out-distanced every one in his year.' But he lacked any strong guidance for the development of his character and any inner restraint upon his temper. One day in the dining-hall at St John's he got into a quarrel with a friend and threw a knife at him. Fortunately, he missed; it stuck quivering in the wall-panelling.

Far away in Cornwall both his father and his younger

sister, Sally, knew that all was not well with him in spite of his academic successes. They prayed for him and tried to help by their letters.

Kempthorne was also uneasy about Henry and suggested to him one day that he ought to be studying not just to win the praises of other people, but for the glory of God. Henry thought the idea reasonable in its way, but rather strange and intangible. It lay half forgotten in the back of his mind when he went home to Truro for the summer vacation in 1799. His father was probably not articulate enough in these matters to say much to a son who had a wider educational experience than his own. But with Sally it was different, and Henry recalled, 'I was frequently addressed by my dear sister on the subject of religion.' He was not inclined to pay much attention to her. In fact his selfishness and irritability seemed to increase while he was at home: 'I spoke in the harshest language to my sister and even to my father, if he happened to differ from my mind and will. What an example of patience and mildness he was! I love to think of his excellent qualities.' Sally managed to extract from him a half-hearted promise to read the Bible, but he did not keep it. So her prayers and efforts to help him appeared to have been rather unsuccessful when he left in October for his third year at Cambridge. At parting, his father was 'in great health and spirits', and when he heard at the end of 1799 that his son had come first in the examinations, he was overjoyed.

Henry decided not to make the long and expensive journey back to Cornwall at Christmas, so he was still in Cambridge in the first days of the new century when a letter came from his half-brother, John, to tell him that their father had suddenly died. It was a stunning blow. He was not quite nineteen and both his parents were dead.

'I was extremely low-spirited and began to consider

13

seriously that invisible world to which he had gone and to which I must one day go. As I had no taste at this time for my usual studies, I took up my Bible. Nevertheless I often took up other books and should have continued to do so had not Kempthorne advised me to make this time an occasion for serious reflection. I began with the Acts, as being the most amusing, and when I was entertained with the narrative I found myself insensibly led to enquire more attentively into the doctrine of the Apostles. On the first night after that I began to pray from a precomposed form, in which I thanked God in general for having sent Christ into the world. But though I prayed for pardon I had little sense of my own sinfulness. Nevertheless I began to consider myself a religious man. When I went to the College chapel I saw, with some surprise at my former inattention, that in the Magnificat there was a great degree of joy expressed at the coming of Christ.'

Kempthorne lent him a book, Doddridge's *Rise and Progress of Religion in the Soul*, but it was more than he could cope with at that stage. 'My proud and wicked heart could not bear to be brought down into the dust.' Yet he was soon writing to tell Sally, 'I am brought to a sense of things gradually. There is nothing particularly striking in it. I began to attend more diligently to the words of our Saviour in the New Testament and to devour them with delight.' Reading of God's free offer of mercy and forgiveness through Jesus Christ, he prayed that he too might share in it. At the time he could not quite find words to express what occurred, but it is evident that, from then on, Christ took the central place in his life as his Saviour and Lord.

Henry was again top in the examinations at the end of his third year. 'Notwithstanding his unassuming manners and almost childlike simplicity,' said one of his contemporaries, 'Martyn was perhaps superior in mental capacity to any one of his day in the University.' Yet the pressure of work was so intense that he was himself surprised that he survived as a Christian, that the tiny spark of life the Holy Spirit had kindled in his heart was not extinguished. He could only thank God for his mercy, and for Kempthorne's friendship, and for Sally too. 'What a blessing it is that I have such a sister as you, my dear, who have been instrumental in keeping me in the right way. How little human assistance you have had and yet to what great knowledge you have attained in religion.' He told her he felt he could now agree with her in most of her opinions.

But there was no relief for the moment from intense concentration on his studies. His final exams came in January 1801, one year after his conversion and just before his twentieth birthday. Though he seemed to himself a stagnant kind of Christian, he did not relax his academic work, and succeeded in maintaining his position as the outstanding mathematician of his year. Yet he felt strangely dissatisfied: 'I obtained my highest wishes but was surprised to find I had grasped a shadow.'

Cornwall gave him a hero's welcome, but Sally was not so impressed. She had hoped to see him make more spiritual progress. And her prayers were answered, for that summer, free at last from the threat of imminent exams, he experienced for the first time the joy of spending time alone with God. After he returned to Cambridge he started writing her long letters full of ardent faith. 'We are lights in the world. Our lives should manifest our high and heavenly calling. Let us provoke one another to good works and be more and more dead to the world but alive unto God through Jesus Christ.' He also tried to speak about the gospel to fellow students and to others he met in the city. On one occasion he went to the home of a man who was dying and was surprised to find that his daughters were not there. He discovered them in another house, light-heartedly being entertained by a student who was reading a play. 'I rebuked him so sharply and, I am afraid, so intemperately, that a quarrel will perhaps ensue.' However, in later years the man thanked Henry for his words, which had been a factor in drawing him to Christ.

In March 1802 he was chosen to be a Fellow of St John's and gained first prize for a Latin essay, an indication that his special gift was not going to be for mathematics at all. In the long vacation he went on a walking tour of Wales, climbing Snowdon by night. 'I cannot describe the horror of the ascent; the deep darkness, the howling of the wind, the violence of the rain, and the sullen silence of the guide.' He finished up in Cornwall again, where he had stimulating talks with Sally and revelled in the rural scenery. 'The deep solitude of the place favoured meditation and for want of other books I was obliged to read my Bible almost exclusively.'

A main reason, however, for Henry's rapid progress during the first three years of his Christian life was that he had been regularly attending Holy Trinity Church in Cambridge. The minister was the Rev. Charles Simeon, a uniquely gifted preacher, numbered among the greatest England has ever known. Whereas Wesley travelled all over the country for fifty-three years preaching Christ, Simeon remained an indefatigable expositor of the Bible in that one church for fifty-four years. Week by week Henry's convictions and character were shaped by Simeon's teaching, till there grew up between them a warmth of affection and mutual admiration, which fortified Henry all his days. Born in a countryside deeply influenced by Wesley and Walker, drawn to Christ through his father, Sally and Kempthorne, and then trained by Simeon, it was his destiny to carry the gospel to lands Wesley and Simeon never saw and at a price God never asked them to pay.

2 In training with Simeon

Shortly after Henry returned to Cambridge in October 1802 he had a conversation with Simeon which proved decisive for the future course of his life. Simeon had been reading reports sent home by William Carey, the Baptist missionary who had sailed for India nine years earlier. He revealed to Henry how impressed he had been by what Carey had accomplished in that time. By the end of the year it was clear to Henry that God was calling him to be a missionary in India too. He remained in Cambridge throughout 1803 with this ultimate goal constantly in his mind.

Some of his friends strongly disapproved, and Sally wrote to say that she thought he was unfit for such a task, 'lacking that deep and solid experience necessary in a missionary'. So, even though he felt God was guiding him, his plans for the future became a constant source of anxiety. He made approaches to the Church Missionary Society, in the foundation of which Simeon had shared in 1799, but from the start there was uncertainty whether he should go to India with the society or in some secular capacity. Then from time to time it was China which attracted him, for at that period there was not a single Protestant missionary there.

Pulled this way and that by his own thoughts and other people's opinions, Henry began to realize that Sally's estimate of his spiritual state was not far wrong. Working with Simeon, dining with Simeon, riding with Simeon to meetings in the villages, he was thrilled with the reality of Christian fellowship. But as he walked back to his lodgings one night after hearing a sermon from Thomas Thomason, Simeon's admirable curate, Henry realized how superficial his own Christian experience had been. Listening to Simeon's preaching, as he did month after month, was even worse: 'Mr Simeon's sermon showed me my corruption and vileness more than any I ever heard.'

It was almost invariably like that. The message of the gospel was expounded so effectively that it struck home, and Henry found his own heart revealed and then helped. 'In the evening Mr Simeon preached a most convincing sermon on the second chapter of Mark. I could not but feel my need of a physician, such as Jesus.' At that time Simeon was just twice Henry's age and they dined together on his forty-fourth birthday, when Henry was amazed to hear him thank God for his creation but ask his forgiveness for having accomplished so little in his life. Henry hoped and prayed he might be half as effective as Simeon was.

Daily Henry was battered by all sorts of personal problems. To accustom himself to self-examination, to improve his soul and his Christian obedience, he began to keep a journal. It was not meant to be a diary, recording events, though fortunately it gradually took on this secondary character too. It was a searingly frank account of his inner state, in which he daily analysed and chastised himself, never content, never pleased with his progress and activities. The discipline of writing it sharpened his literary style, so that in spite of its introspective tone, scarcely a page lacked penetrating insights and memorable expressions. All his struggles and failures were recorded, though he often seemed unconscious of the rapid advances he was making at the same time. Up to 1803 we have but scant data about Henry, but from the moment he started the journal there is a spotlight on the man behind the events.

Unfortunately it survives today only in printed form, and we have no means of knowing what the editor omitted. For the whole Cambridge period of his life the journal is almost totally lacking in descriptions of any kind. The names of Henry's friends and contacts are left out, replaced by a dash, or at best an initial. We learn next to nothing about his physical circumstances. The journal majors on self-examination, on prayer, the Bible and preaching. It is particularly disappointing that it contains not a single account of Simeon, so that we can build up no realistic picture of Henry's relationship with him or with John Sargent, his closest student friend. Such concrete details as can be scraped together about his life at Cambridge come mainly from those who wrote long afterwards.

With India as the great objective ahead, it was decided that Henry should be ordained and become a second curate to Simeon, but this was no simple matter for him to contemplate. He was dismayed to find that, for fear of what some of his friends would think, he was ashamed to admit he was joining Simeon. Nor did he seem to himself to be in the right state of mind for such a step. While he faithfully attended the Communion services at Holy Trinity Church, they left him unsatisfied: 'I received the sacrament but I fear I do not understand the nature of it, as I never derive benefit from it. My heart was hard and I knew not what to do.' And at that time even just talking with people generally left him ruffled: 'I lack a sense of God's presence when I am with others.' In spite of his great academic successes, he was still only twenty-two and more immature than either he or his best friends realized. Brought up in a remote corner of England, and lacking any positive Christian guidance until his third year at Cambridge, he had barely had time to get adjusted to the responsibilities which now descended upon him.

On Sunday, 23 October 1803 he was ordained in Ely Cathedral. He did not enjoy the ceremony, feeling ashamed that so ignorant and unholy a person as he should be offering himself for the ministry of the Lord Jesus Christ. After dinner he walked straight back to Cambridge, a distance of sixteen miles, and went at once to Holy Trinity Church to begin his work. At night when he knelt to pray he was violently sick: 'In the pain and disorder of my body I could but commend myself faintly to God's mercy in Jesus Christ.'

It was part of his duty to ride out to the village of Lolworth each week, so he was immediately faced with the ordeal of preaching there on Sunday, 30 October. He had never preached a sermon in his life. He had had no training in a theological college. All he had to guide him was the experience of listening to Simeon and Thomason, both of them good preachers. But to do it himself was quite another thing. All that first week he struggled to prepare the sermon, feeling very depressed. His text proved to be from the book of Job, 'If a man die, shall he live again?' Afterwards one of his hearers sat with him for two hours, arguing that his ideas about missionary work were due to youthful enthusiasm and that he had the strength of neither mind nor body for such work.

Preparing for the second Sunday at Lolworth seemed a little easier, until the morning of the day: 'I was in a very happy frame of mind at the thought of preaching the gospel, but on reading over my sermon I was chilled and frozen by the deadness and stupidity of it.' It was too late to do anything but commit himself into God's hands and ride off. The congregation was very small and he was thankful when it was all over. Then an old man walked for some distance beside his horse, advising him to keep praying, to tell people they were sinners, and to put Christ before himself. He never forgot it.

That same evening, back in Cambridge, he read the Prayer Book service at Holy Trinity Church before Simeon preached. This was less of an ordeal, but to his dismay people told him afterwards that they could not hear him properly and that he must read with more solemnity and better elocution. He felt very depressed: 'I began to see for the first time that I must be content to take my place among men of second-rate ability and that there were others who excelled me in everything.'

Being on Simeon's staff involved other tasks for which he found himself equally ill-equipped. 'The work of visiting the people of Cambridge, reading the Bible to them, and praying with them, appeared hateful to me,' he confessed, only one month after his ordination, 'but through God's grace my self-will did not prevail. I called today at three of the parishioners' houses and found them all in the most profound state of ignorance and stupidity.'

It was a good thing he retained some secular duties as well. For three years he was examiner at St John's College, not in mathematics as one might have supposed, but in the classics. This compelled him to give time to reading Euripedes and Aeschylus, Butler and Locke, Pindar, Thucydides and Xenophon. 'Did I delight in reading of the retreat of the ten thousand Greeks and shall not my soul glory in the knowledge of God who created the Greeks and the vast countries over which they passed?' In very different circumstances he was to pass that way himself in due time.

Sermon preparation, Sunday duties, tutoring, examining, visiting parishioners and the sick, and his own strenuous programme of study crowded his days. 'The business of life leaves me far too little time for meditation, so that I

know little of God and my own soul. My extreme emptiness must be due to not reading more of God's Word,
which I have therefore determined to do, for it is more
important than the duties of the ministry, which I cannot
perform well without it. So I passed this rainy morning in
studying Hebrew and reading the Epistle to the Philip-
pians in Greek.' The Hebrew Old Testament and the
Greek New Testament became part of his daily diet, not
something he had to force himself into, but a pure delight
in which he revelled.

And he not only read the Bible and prayed with an
intensity few could match, he also began to learn whole
passages of Scripture by heart – Paul's discourse to the
Ephesian elders in the Acts of the Apostles, many of the
Psalms, and a good part of the First Epistle to Timothy,
for 'now that I am in the ministry these instructions
affect me in a different way'. He never refers to learning
individual verses, it was always large sections of the Bible.
'I read the fourth and fifth chapters of the First Epistle to
the Thessalonians with exceeding profit and learnt them
by heart. . . . I addressed myself with earnest prayer to
know and learn the Epistle to the Romans, in Greek.'

Of course there were critics of all this. One friend told
him that by immoderate seclusion he was deadening
those fine feelings which we should all cultivate, and
neglecting the active duties of life. He maintained that so
thorough a change of heart and behaviour was not
necessary to make us Christians. 'His amazing volubility
left me unable to say anything, but I kept my temper
pretty well.' And the critic probably little knew the
versatility of his man, for Henry could claim that 'since I
have known God in a saving manner, painting, poetry
and music have had charms unknown to me before. I
have received what I suppose is a taste for them, but
religion has refined my mind and made it susceptible to
the sublime and the beautiful. My heart adores the Lord

as the creator of all fair scenes, as the source of all the intellectual beauty which delights me, and as the former of the mind which can find pleasure in beauty.'

At the year's end he prayed for strength to fit him for a long life of warfare and self-denial, for light at dark times of trouble, and that he might not shrink from any painful labour for Christ's sake. His prayer was to be granted in full, except for the word 'long'.

It fell to him after Christmas to conduct the marriage ceremony for a couple who were sincere believers. He greatly enjoyed it, yet admitted, 'I felt thankful that I was delivered from all desires for the comforts of married life. With the most desirable partner and every prospect of happiness, I would prefer a single life in which there are much greater opportunities for heavenly-mindedness.'

3 The steep ascent

In search of the best way of getting to India, Henry spent ten days in London early in 1804. He wanted to meet Charles Grant, a well-known evangelical leader, who was Chairman of the Board of Directors of the East India Company. Free from normal duties he spent the whole of his first morning in the capital studying the Greek New Testament and then walked to India House in Leadenhall Street. Grant suggested they take the coach to Clapham to see William Wilberforce. On the way they talked about India, and Grant told Henry that Bengali was the language in widest use there, but that the lingua franca of the English settlements was Hindustani – or Urdu, as we would say today – a mixture of several languages including Arabic, Persian and Sanskrit.

They reached Wilberforce's home for dinner and spent the evening in wide-ranging conversation about India, Australia, and the authority of the church, a subject raised by a priest who was present, whom Henry addressed in French. It was a wonderful experience for him to meet men of such wide intellectual and spiritual horizons as Grant and Wilberforce. They even suggested he might take over the Anglican church in Calcutta. At night Wilberforce gathered his large household together, read to them from the Bible, explained what he had read, and prayed. Henry stayed the night and talked with him alone next morning. Then he took the coach back to London, speaking to the driver about the gospel all the way.

Though a little uneasy in the bustle of the great city, he took the chance of visiting the British Museum several times, attended a lecture on music, called on remarkable old John Newton, hymn-writer and former slave-trader, and attended a valedictory meeting for two German missionaries. 'I shook their hands and almost wished to go with them.'

Back in Cambridge he was face to face again with the weekly task of preparing sermons and penetrating the dull minds of the rustics of Lolworth, 'as ignorant of the gospel as heathen'. In the cold, snowy weather he had to fight against a strong dislike of going there at all. They seemed incapable of comprehending what he said, so he was often dejected on his Sunday rides, wondering how he would manage in India since he found the English so difficult to teach. But he prayed. At times he fasted and prayed. On his twenty-third birthday, 'in prayer at noon I interceded seriously for the people of Lolworth, asking that I might take delight in being with them and wait in faith for this wilderness to blossom as the rose.'

Indeed, Cambridge and the University had transformed him. He had been there almost seven years. He had become a Christian there, but he had also become a different kind of human being altogether. He was no longer a country boy. Meeting some of the great men of the time, like Grant and Wilberforce, he had felt completely at home: they had immediately communicated to him and he to them. He belonged to their world now, rather than to the villages. In fact ever since that talk with Grant on the Clapham coach a new dimension had been added to his work. It sprang up everywhere in his journal: 'After breakfast I read Urdu for three hours. . . . After dinner I prayed with two sick persons and on my return finished the Bengali grammar. . . . I spent the morning reading an Arabic grammar. . . . A funeral took

25

up my time till eleven, then I made some calculations in trigonometry and read Persian.' All this in addition to Hebrew, Greek and Latin.

At the same time Henry plunged into other kinds of exacting training for the future in India. 'I sat down in the evening to read the Scriptures for my own comfort and was able to give many hours to it uninterruptedly. I collected all the passages from the four gospels which had any reference to self-denial. It is a subject I need to preach to myself and to others. How unspeakably awful is the latter part of the ninth chapter of Mark. I resolved on my knees to live a life of far more self-denial than I have ever yet done and to begin with little things. Accordingly, I ate my breakfast standing at a distance from the fire and stood reading at the window during the morning, though the thermometer was at freezing point. I was so cold I did not get on much with my sermon, but the effect on the flow of my thoughts was surprising, the tone and vigour of my mind rose rapidly. No difficulty daunted me. I rejoiced that God had made this life a time of trial. To climb the steep ascent, to run, to fight, to wrestle, was the strong desire of my heart.'

During this formative period in his life, Henry's hero was David Brainerd, the young minister who became a missionary to the American Indians in the days when the advancing European settlers were pushing them out of their homelands. 'I thought of David Brainerd and ardently desired his devotedness to God. I feel my heart knit to this dear man. I long to be like him. Let me forget the world and be swallowed up in a desire to glorify God.' Brainerd's personal devotion to Christ and the self-sacrificing way in which he endured hardship in the service of others made a great appeal to Henry. He modelled his life on Brainerd's, so that, to some extent, their attitudes and careers ran parallel.

Winter passed into spring. He composed poetry, baptized a few children, visited the dying, took daily exercise, and rebuked a group of people who were quarrelling in the street. Four times a day he knelt in prayer, yet never felt he prayed enough. 'Not a day passes without annoyances. Every day my will is thwarted. I seem to pray to a God not angry, but indifferent to my prayers. Yet on the spot where I have often found the presence of God, the scene of many sacred thoughts, my Bethel, I knelt down and prayed for relief for my soul.'

May came and he walked out one morning before breakfast, 'the beauties of the opening spring constraining me to adoration. I took my paper and ink into the garden, looking up to God for assistance, and wrote freely for two hours.' Yet those sermons at which he toiled rarely seemed to come off as well as he hoped: 'My preaching falls infinitely short of what I should call good.' And when his words *were* appreciated, his self-criticism remained so rigorous that he would not allow himself the luxury of satisfaction: 'They all talked in praise of my sermon on Sunday, but praise is exceedingly unpleasant to me, because I am slow to render back to God that glory which belongs to him alone. Sometimes it may be useful in encouraging me, but in truth, praise generally produces pride, and pride sets me far from God.' No matter what happened he refused to consider his Christian life or service a success. He remained a penitent, convinced of his own corruption and inadequacy. So acute was his inner conflict and his sense of unworthiness that he was tempted to say, 'I often regret that I am not a private Christian.'

And all the time Simeon was beside him, so stable and strong, always encouraging him in their talks together, always marvellously effective in his preaching. 'Mr Simeon spoke on the words "My meat is to do the will of him that sent me and to finish his work". My soul was stirred within me to follow the Lord's steps and devote

27

myself entirely to his service, as I do not believe I had ever truly done before. I almost trembled to promise God I would be his servant for ever, but I gave myself up to him in prayer to be a follower of Jesus Christ.'

In June Simeon and Henry rode out together to the village where Thomason lived. All the way Simeon talked to him about India, suggesting he should sail early in 1805. It was not because he wanted to get rid of Henry, but simply that he regarded the proclamation of the gospel in Asia as part of his duty and encouraged the gifted young men whom he attracted to obey the command of the Lord Jesus Christ to make him known to everyone in the world.

In fact Simeon was deeply attached to Henry, whom he had known since his conversion in 1800. In Henry, Simeon found the son he never had. In Simeon, Henry found the father he had lost. Simeon was alive to Henry's limitations and immaturities. He advised him and he criticized him; but basically he did not at all share Henry's derogatory view of himself. All his life Simeon regarded Henry with awe as well as affection, marvelling at the God-given gifts he saw emerging in him, and rejoicing at what these could mean for the spread of the gospel in India.

Simeon's original hope, and Henry's, had been that the latter would go to India as a plain missionary, 'poor as the Lord and his apostles', but on financial grounds it seemed desirable that he should become a chaplain with the East India Company and draw a better salary than the Church Missionary Society could possibly pay him. His half-brother John had a large family and it is probable that difficulties arose over their father's will. When he was ordained, Henry forfeited his share of the inheritance. Although Sally had married a Mr Pearson, she too was in financial difficulties, and Henry felt an obligation to provide for her. Then came the problem of his landlady at Cambridge, who was married to a clergyman.

One day Henry threw open the door of his room and crashed it into her face with disastrous results. He set aside a considerable sum to give her an annuity, from which she profited for the rest of her long life.

The combination of these factors inclined Henry to go out with the East India Company. Even so the news of what he was intending to do came as a severe shock to many of his academic acquaintances. One evening some important person joined him as he walked, and said that 'he thought it a most improper step for me to leave the University in order to preach to the ignorant heathen, which any person could do, and that I ought to improve the opportunity of acquiring human learning. All our conversation ended in nothing. He was convinced he was right, and according to him the texts of Scripture I produced were applicable only to the time of the apostles.'

He was awarded his Master of Arts degree in the senate house at Cambridge in July, and about the same time passed through a brief ordeal, unique in his experience. One night when he was praying, 'God either showed me myself, or else Satan tempted me to commit his own sin. My soul was filled with misery and horror. I don't know how to describe my feelings, or how I got into them, but it was after metaphysical enquiries into the nature and end of my being. My thoughts were those of cool, deliberate pride, a sort of calm rejection of the authority of God and of the necessity for humiliation before him. I was afraid to stop praying lest I should sink down with the devil and his angels, whose spirit of rebellion I seemed to have obtained. Next day these distressing, atheist thoughts returned to fill my soul with anguish, but after an hour spent in prayer the Lord mercifully assisted me. With great difficulty, forcing my way through the crowd of enemies within, and I think also Satan without, I commended my soul to Christ. Such thoughts dishonour the

Saviour and deny his authority, tearing me away from my best and only Friend. Yet they shall not, if Christ give me grace to stand firm.'

And then it was time for a two-month vacation in Cornwall. The journey took about a week each way. He had not been home for two years, and this was to be his last visit to Laura and Sally and his relatives before he sailed for India in the spring. So it was with a sense of joy and relief that he rode back to Cambridge from Lolworth through a tremendous storm on the evening of 8 July 1804. Next morning he took the coach for London. He made full use of his one day there. Grant warned him that because of the war situation there might be delays before he could sail. He had a meal with his close friend, John Sargent, one day to be his biographer. Sargent told him 'of his approaching marriage to a lady of uncommon excellence, which rather excited in me a desire after a similar state, but I strove against it'. And the next meal was with Wilberforce, who took him to the House of Commons to hear William Pitt make a speech. Henry was delighted at his eloquence and only wished the Prime Minister's powers of oratory were 'employed in recommending the gospel'.

On the Wednesday he left London for Bath. His seat was up on the top of the coach in a bitterly cold wind, so it was an unpleasant trip. He was 'most dreadfully assailed by evil thoughts, but at the very height prayer prevailed and I was delivered and during the rest of the journey enjoyed great peace and a strong desire to live for Christ alone, forsaking marriage and the pleasures of the world'. On 12 July he reached Exeter. On the 13th he was in Plymouth, where he stayed three nights with his cousin, Tom Hitchins, who had married a girl named Emma Grenfell from Marazion, near Penzance in Cornwall. On 16 July he came to Truro and his own people. The visit was to be of crucial importance in his life.

4 The beloved idol

Henry made his way at once to Sally's home outside
Truro, where the River Fal ran into an arm of the sea.
Her husband was vicar of two villages, Lamorran and
St Michael Penkevil. Their house at Lamorran looked
down over a narrow strip of water to wooded hills on the
south.

This was home to him as much as any place since
his father's death, and he was in and out a good deal
during the next seven weeks. His sister Laura did not
really share that faith in Christ which bound him and
Sally together, though he had a long talk with her about
it. And he found himself just a little disappointed in
Sally. As they walked to Truro 'I told her gently that she
was not adorning the doctrine of God by a cheerful and
contented temper. She was in tears. I went on my way
afraid that I had not been tender enough.'

But he had not just been thinking of Laura and Sally
on that long trip to Cornwall. On Saturday, 28 July he
rode on westwards for another twenty-five miles to the
village of St Hilary, above Mount's Bay, not far short of
Penzance. On the Sunday morning in church at St
Hilary, 'my thoughts wandered from the service and I
suffered the keenest disappointment. Lydia Grenfell did
not come. Yet, in great pain, I thanked God for having
kept her away, as she might have been a snare to me.'
But that same afternoon he walked a mile and a half to
Marazion, opposite St Michael's Mount, called at the

31

Grenfell home, and went out with Lydia and someone else, 'conversing on spiritual subjects'.

That was enough. Back at St Hilary 'all the rest of the evening and at night I could not keep her out of my mind. I felt too plainly that I loved her passionately. The direct opposition of this to my devotedness to God in the missionary way excited no small tumult in my mind. At night I continued an hour and a half in prayer, striving against this attachment. I endeavoured to analyse it, that I might see how worthless such love to a speck of earth was when compared with divine love. Then I read the most solemn parts of Scripture. One while I was about to triumph, but in a moment my heart had wandered to the beloved idol. I went to bed in great pain, yet still rather superior to the enemy, but in dreams her image returned and I woke in the night with my mind full of her.'

And so, on one holiday Sunday in the summer, a speck of earth, the beloved idol, moved into the centre of Henry's thinking to challenge his conceptions of self-denial and his call to India. With so radical a departure coming in sight he was, of course, peculiarly susceptible, but next morning he rose in great peace. 'God seemed to have caused the tempest of self-will to subside.' Resolutely he rode off, away from Marazion, fifteen miles back to Gwennap, his father's family home, meditating on the eighth chapter of the Epistle to the Romans. He then went to Redruth, and 'on the road I was enabled to triumph at last and found my heart as pleased as ever with the prospect of a single life in missionary labours'.

For the time being Lydia Grenfell was left to think her own thoughts. She was the younger sister of Emma, his cousin Tom Hitchins' wife, with whom he had recently stayed in Plymouth. She was twenty-nine, six years older than Henry. Since he once remarked that all the happier years of his early life had been spent at St Hilary, we must presume that he had known her in childhood and

32

schooldays, before he went to Cambridge. For although she does not figure in Henry's journal before the July Sunday, it is clear that he went west from Truro deliberately to see her again.

He then returned to Sally and on Sunday morning, 5 August, preached at St Michael Penkevil. Almost all his Christian life had been spent in Cambridge, so it was quite a novelty for the family to see him in the pulpit. 'My two sisters heard me preach for the first time.' Thinking specially of Laura he explained the conversation between Christ and the woman of Samaria. Afterwards she walked back with him to Lamorran and he was delighted to find that she had been deeply affected by his words. In the evening he preached at Lamorran on the parable of the lost sheep and the people seemed to receive his message much better than they had at Lolworth. Late at night he walked alone by the sea, his heart full of praise to God, particularly because of Laura. 'We are now brothers and sisters for eternity.'

At first these two country churches in the care of Sally's husband were the only ones open to him. Otherwise 'the clergy seem to have united to exclude me', for the word had gone round that 'Mr Martyn is a Calvinist preacher in the dissenting way'. Even his old headmaster, Dr Cardew, who had always been so proud of Henry's successes, offered his own services as preacher at any time in order to keep him out of the Cornish pulpits. In spite of that, someone he had breakfast with – probably Sally's husband – 'entered into the highest points of the Calvinist scheme. His views appeared to me unscriptural. My heart was frozen by the conversation and I wanted to leave these things for others more practical. He had but a slight opinion of missionary work and depressed my spirits a little, though I know he has great affection for me.' His spirits were further depressed when a friend in

Truro 'used every argument to dissuade me from going to India, some of them not without weight'.

On Sunday, 19 August, he did get the chance of addressing a very large congregation at Kenwyn, north of Truro. 'The church was quite full, many outside, and many obliged to go away. At first I felt uneasy from the number of people gazing at me, but my peace soon returned and I delivered my sermon.' Then he moved cautiously towards Lydia again.

He spent one whole day walking to St Hilary, learning the Epistle to the Ephesians by heart as he went. Down by the sea he found a large cave in which he meditated and prayed. Lydia was only a mile away but he held off till Sunday, 26 August and then 'rose early and walked out, invited by the beauty of the morning. Many pleasing thoughts crowded on my mind as I viewed the sea, the rocks, the Mount, and the bay, and thought of the person who lived near it.' He waited till evening and then called at the house and 'walked with Mr Grenfell and Lydia up the hill with the most beautiful view of the sea. But I was unhappy, feeling my attachment to Lydia, for I was unwilling to leave her.'

Next day he went back. 'I walked to Marazion with my heart more delivered from its idolatry and enabled to look steadily and peacefully to God.' In the afternoon he sat reading to her and thus they were alone together for the first time. 'Now, thought I, here am I in the presence of God and my idol. I felt cheerfully resigned to do the will of God and to forgo the earthly joy – which I had just been desiring with my whole heart. I continued conversing with her, generally with my heart in heaven, but every now and then resting on her. Then I parted with Lydia, perhaps for ever in this life, with a sort of uncertain pain which I knew would increase to greater violence afterwards. I walked to St Hilary, determining in great tumult to be the servant of God. All the rest of the evening, in company or alone, I could think of nothing but her excellencies.'

Two days later he walked back to Truro, over twenty miles, his mind still taken up with Lydia. There he met a Major Sandys who talked a lot about India and invited him to Helston, half way back to Marazion. He accepted, but then spent two hours in the garden at night, 'reasoning with my perverse heart'.

The evening he reached Helston the curate called. Henry took to him at once 'and tried to give him what I thought were scriptural views of the doctrines of the gospel'. He was asked to preach at the church, but in doing so gave great offence to some of the ladies, who said they would not hear such doctrines a second time. He felt it diplomatic to decline a warm invitation to preach at the Methodist chapel.

He returned the curate's call and 'pressed him closely on leaving off cards, plays, dances, and forsaking the company of the world'. The man seemed convinced of the necessity of devoting himself much more seriously to the service of God and came again next day to say good-bye to Henry and thank him for their talks. Reassured that God had brought him to Helston, Henry did not go on to Marazion, but rode to Redruth and then walked in the night to Truro, 'with my mind generally at peace and rejoicing in God'.

He gave the last two days to Sally at Lamorran. They read the Acts of the Apostles together and he urged her to give herself wholly to God. At the end, 'I exhorted and comforted my sister and then took leave of her with great distress to us both.' They did not expect to meet again on earth.

On his return journey Henry spent three nights with Tom and Emma at Plymouth. Emma told him that his attachment to her sister was not altogether unreturned. 'The discovery gave me both pleasure and pain, but alone at night I resigned myself entirely to the will of God and next morning took leave of this family, who truly have God with them in their house.'

Beyond Exeter he got talking with a lawyer who knew he needed some change in his life. 'While the coach stopped to change horses we went into a garden and sat by some water on the grassy slopes. I read and explained to him the twenty-third Psalm.' One of the other passengers was a prisoner of war out on parole, a young French Protestant who had lost his Bible when he was captured. Henry felt his views of the gospel to be so defective that he talked with him a long time about 'his state by nature, his condemnation by the law, the necessity of regeneration, free salvation by Christ, and the promise of the Spirit'. Later he sent him a French New Testament and for some time they corresponded in French.

After a day in London with Grant, he was back in Cambridge on 15 September for his last few months with Simeon. 'To preach the gospel to my poor fellow-creatures that they might obtain the salvation which is in Christ Jesus' seemed then a glorious calling, and Lydia, 'a small hindrance'.

He found the city a dreary wilderness at first, after the freedom and distractions of Cornwall. He went round the hospital wards, speaking to the patients about Christ. He struggled to control children and teach them the gospel, and discovered he could do both. He was heavily involved in the end of the year examinations at St John's, and all the corners of his time were filled in by the study of Urdu and Bengali. One November day was typical of the pressures upon him: a student came to breakfast and for two hours Henry helped him in mathematics; then he visited a dying woman and prayed with her family; other students came to be tutored in the classics; 'a disagreeable man took up my time after dinner', then came a class of children, more tutoring in classics, and no leisure till the evening, which was spent preparing his sermon for Lolworth. On reaching the place next day he faced a mere ten people in church, and the meeting was suddenly brought to a close when a man fainted during the sermon and had to be carried out. In the open air, while the man revived, Henry was told that his 'preaching would not do at all for this place, as the language was seldom such as the people could understand'. But he did not give up. His sense of the call of Christ, along with the people's obvious ignorance and need, held him. Yet his contacts with them were too limited, and his time around Cambridge too short, for him to master the problems and see any real answer to his prayers.

Letters from Laura were disappointing, as they contained no Christian reference at all. Henry felt that an evil spirit was deceiving her. 'For my dear sister I wrestled in prayer with more earnestness than I have yet done for anyone.'

Sally was not a good correspondent, and etiquette forbade letters between him and Lydia. As time passed he could reflect more calmly on the brief hours he had spent with her on those three days in July and August. He was pleased when Simeon showed him a letter from Calcutta saying, 'Let him marry and come out at once', but it did not alter his resolve to sail single. Nor did the appearance of John Sargent, passing through Cambridge to his wedding. 'After supper I sat with him at the inn. Even with all the blessings Sargent is about to possess, I rejoice exceedingly in what the Lord has allotted to me. I feel no wish to live except to be employed in that work for which Christ died.'

At the dawn of 1805 Henry looked back on the days of his youth as mere child's play, just training for the big task ahead: 'So closes the easy part of my life. I may be said scarcely to have experienced trouble, but now – farewell ease. O Lord, into thy hands I commend my spirit.'

For the present he had to learn to live with uncertainty. In January, Grant told him to stand by to sail in ten days' time. But it was illegal for him to be ordained priest till he was twenty-four on 18 February, so that crisis passed, and Simeon suggested it might be ten weeks before he could go. He advised Henry not to get settled near Calcutta in case he was drawn into institutions where he would be 'more than half a secular man'. He wanted him to break clear from European company in Asia and reach the thinkers and leaders of society in their own languages and cultures. As the men talked in Simeon's rooms at King's College, these seed thoughts took root in Henry's mind, and were to shape the development of his life.

However, it became impossible to give proper attention to his work at Trinity Church; out of his last thirteen weeks as Simeon's curate, five were spent in London. He was often with Grant at India House. Dr Gilchrist the orientalist, who had been a colleague of Carey's in Calcutta, helped him with Urdu, in which he made such rapid strides that he began to dream of trying his hand at translating the New Testament. Gilchrist wisely told him to wait till he knew the language a lot better and had lived some years in India. And on Sundays he preached for the Rev. Richard Cecil at St John's Chapel in Bedford Row. Indeed, Cecil proved an excellent friend for Henry, though he could be even blunter than Simeon in his criticisms. 'After I had preached, Mr Cecil said a great deal to me on the necessity of gaining the attention of the people and speaking with more warmth and earnestness. I felt wounded a little at finding myself to have failed in so many things, yet I succeeded in coming down to the dust and received gladly the kind advice of wise friends.'

On Sunday, 10 March 1805 he was ordained priest in the Chapel Royal at St James's in London. Sailing dates could not be fixed because of the imminent threat of invasion by Napoleon's forces, poised within sight across the Channel. So it was decided he should move from Cambridge to London to be available to leave at any moment. He went back for a final three-day visit. 'I supped with Simeon alone. He prayed before I went away, and my heart was deeply moved.'

Sunday, 7 April was his last day. In the morning he preached at Lolworth. 'An old farmer, as he was taking leave of me, turned aside to shed tears, and this affected me more than anything. I rode away with a heavy heart, partly at my own corruption, partly at leaving this place in such general hardness of heart. I prayed over the whole of my sermon for the evening at Trinity and when I came to preach it, God assisted me beyond my hopes. Most of the younger people seemed to be in tears. Mr Simeon commended me to God in prayer, in which among other things he pleaded for a richer blessing on my soul. He perceives that I need it, and so do I. Professor Farish walked home with me to the College gate and there I parted from him with no small sorrow.'

Early next morning the students were round at Henry's place. He longed to be alone and pray, but it was impossible. 'A great many accompanied me to the coach. It was a thick, misty morning so the University with its towers and spires was out of sight in an instant.'

He never came back.

5 The struggle to leave

The dangerous war situation, the ever-present possibility
of invasion, and conflicting reports about the movement
of hostile French and Spanish fleets out of their Atlantic
ports, delayed Henry for another three months, all of
which he spent in London. On 24 April he was officially
appointed chaplain to the East India Company, taking
the oath at India House in the presence of all the directors and with Grant in the chair.

The Archbishop of Canterbury granted him an interview at Lambeth Palace. 'He spoke much on the importance of the work, the small ecclesiastical establishment in
India for so great a population, and the state of the English there who, he said, "called themselves Christians".
He was very civil to me and wished me every success.'
Less formal and more memorable was a second visit to
John Newton. 'He made several striking remarks about
my work. He said he had heard of a clever gardener who
would sow his seeds when the meat was put in to roast
and promise to produce a salad by the time it was ready,
but the Lord did not sow oaks in this way. On my saying
that perhaps I should never live to see much fruit, he
answered that I should have a bird's-eye view of it, which
would be better. When I referred to the opposition I was
likely to meet with he said he supposed Satan would not
love me for what I was about to do. The old man prayed
afterwards with sweet simplicity.' And all these things
came about.

Cecil continued to give him opportunities to preach, and to criticize him when he had done so. 'I went to Mr Cecil's to tea. As usual he was very striking in his observations and I sat contented to be despised. I thank the Lord that he has placed me for a time in London, where so many friends are endeavouring to correct me. I feel encouraged to make every effort to become an able minister of the New Testament. This is one of the benefits of my delay in England.' But he always found the big city difficult after Cambridge. 'How many temptations there are in the streets of London. I made a covenant with my eyes, which I kept strictly, though I was astonished to find the difficulty I had in doing this.'

One night in June he 'sat and meditated and prayed, for I was too fatigued to kneel. My dear Redeemer is a fountain of life to my soul. May I from this time be his, encouraged by his kind promises, and walk in his love under the guidance of his Spirit. With resignation and peace I can look forward to a life of labour and entire seclusion from earthly comforts, while Jesus stands near me. With the Bible in my hand and Christ at my right hand strengthening me, I can do all things.'

But his resignation and peace were about to be shattered: 'Tonight I have been thinking much of Lydia. Memory has been at work to unnerve my soul. But reason, honour, and love to Christ shall prevail. Amen. God help me.' On top of his own thoughts came Cecil declaring 'very strongly and freely that I should be acting like a madman if I went to India unmarried'. That evening a whole group of his friends turned out to be enthusiastic advocates of his marriage, 'yet Mr Atkinson, whose opinion I revere, was against it and I myself felt as cold as an anchorite on the subject'. For a week he was tormented by different opinions, so he wrote a long letter to Simeon asking for his advice. 'May the Lord suggest something to him to guide me.' While he waited for the answer he was pulled first one way then the other, almost hourly. 'How the discussion of this subject has opened all my wounds afresh. I have not felt such heart-rending pain since I parted from her in Cornwall.'

When Simeon's reply came, 'I was immediately convinced beyond doubt of the expediency of celibacy'. He read it to Cecil and the others: all appeared to agree. 'So I devoted myself once more to the everlasting service of God, though my heart was sometimes ready to break with agony. Such is the conflict. Why have my friends mentioned this subject?'

Then all was swallowed up in actual steps towards departure. He packed, and sent off his luggage. There was a farewell party at Grant's, when he was embarrassed to find himself the centre of so much interest. He had his portrait painted by a woman who argued strongly against his Christian faith. After hours of dispute Henry felt it right to warn her that God's judgment would fall on those who rejected the gospel. He spent a last evening with Wilberforce. John Thornton, the famous Christian business man, took him to the Admiralty to take leave of old Lord Barham, whom Pitt had installed there. And he was greatly encouraged by several talks with Daniel Corrie, a fellow student from Cambridge, who revealed that he too expected to serve Christ in India. After his last sermon at St John's many crowded round him in kindly affection. 'How little do people know what inward loneliness there is with all this bustle and noise about my going abroad.'

He left London on 8 July, spent that night at Alton in Hampshire, and on the 9th visited Sargent, the newly-wed, at Midhurst in Sussex, riding back to Petersfield that night. 'As I was undressing I fainted and fell into a convulsive fit. I lost my senses for a time and on recovering found myself in intense pain. I slept very little.' He does not seem to have had a medical overhaul to test his fitness for service in Asia. In later times he would probably not have passed if he had.

At Portsmouth on 10 July Henry boarded his ship, *The Union*. She was part of a fleet whose route was unknown and whose departure was delayed for a week in hope of news of Nelson's return from the West Indies. A good many of Henry's friends from Cambridge and London were there to see him off, among them Simeon and Sargent, who knew that it was his determination to live and die in Asia, and that 'he left England for Christ's sake and he left it for ever'. On Sunday Henry preached to the crew in the morning and Simeon preached at night. They sang hymns by moonlight, and there was no lack of warm affection and prayer. As was his way at a long parting, Simeon took Henry's hand in both of his, and early on 17 July the commander fired the signal gun and the convoy headed for the open sea. Before long Henry was horribly sea-sick.

For the next forty-eight hours the fleet moved slowly westwards, past Plymouth, and along the coast of Devon. On the morning of 19 July, to his utter astonishment, Henry found himself gazing at Cornwall, and the whole convoy came to anchor in Falmouth harbour. 'I seemed to be entirely at home, the scene about me so familiar, and my friends so near. I was rather flurried at the singularity of this providence of God.' Truro, Lamorran and Sally were close at hand. Lydia was only twenty-five miles away.

The very next day Napoleon ordered the embarkation of his invasion force at Boulogne and other Channel ports. If the wind blew from the south the French fleets might at any moment pour out of the Atlantic harbours to hold the narrow seas, while the transports landed in Kent. And Nelson was still not back. In this great national crisis Henry's convoy was held at Falmouth for the next three weeks.

From the first he longed to go to Lydia, 'but I dare not; let the Lord open the way if it is his will'. But after a week he could bear it no longer. Early on 25 July he boarded the mail coach from Falmouth and 'arrived at Marazion in time for breakfast and met my beloved Lydia'. He was totally unexpected. 'In the course of the morning I walked with her, though not uninterruptedly. With much confusion I declared my affection for her with the intention of learning whether, if ever I saw it right in India to be married, she would come out. But she would not declare her sentiments. She said the shortness of arrangements was an obstacle, even if all others were removed. In great tumult I walked up to St Hilary. After dinner I returned to Mr Grenfell's, but on account of the number of persons there I had no opportunity of being alone with Lydia.'

Her own account of these events reveals a somewhat different viewpoint: 'I was surprised this morning by a visit from H.M. I have passed the day chiefly with him. The distance he is going, and the errand he is going on, rendered his society particularly interesting. I felt as if bidding a final adieu to him in this world, and all he said was as the words of one on the borders of eternity. May the Lord moderate the sorrows I feel at parting with so valuable and excellent a friend. Some pains have attended it, known only to God and myself. May we each pursue our different paths and meet at last around our Father's throne.' Next day she added, 'Lord, deliver me from this temptation, help me to conquer my natural feelings. Dare I desire what thou dost plainly, by thy providence, condemn?'

On Sunday, back in Falmouth, Henry preached both at the church and on board *The Union*. He also walked to Lamorran to see Sally. But, though others knew nothing of it, he had been deeply disturbed by the encounter with Lydia. 'The consequence of my Marazion journey is that I am enveloped in gloom and that I love Lydia more than ever.' Gloomy or not, Henry lost no opportunity of trying out his Urdu on the Indian sailors. At first they greeted him with indifference. 'I asked them if they knew who Jesus Christ was. They said, No. I told them he came into the world to save sinners. They smiled, saying, Well, well.' Then it was thought they might be involved in action against the French at any moment. Battle stations were allocated. Everyone was disturbed. A surgeon assured Henry he had never committed any sin. An officer slipped a note into his hand asking for spiritual help. The carpenter complained he had never yet known what it was to be happy: 'I pointed out to him the path of life, in which he would soon be happy.' As a violent gale struck the convoy a depressed corporal was chatting on deck with Henry: 'I tried to revive him and by doing so refreshed myself. We stood together looking wistfully at the raging sea.'

It was a relief to get on shore next day. Henry was fascinated by the faces and the ways of the Indians as they rowed him from the ship. 'I longed to know their language so as to preach the gospel to them. I looked forward with great pleasure to living among them.' The gale hit Marazion too. 'It is a stormy, tempestuous night,' wrote Lydia, 'and this evening I have had many fears concerning an absent friend. Lord, do thou regulate the apprehensions of affection and make me acquiesce in whatever is thy will.'

But in spite of the strong wind from the south, the French fleets did not put to sea. *The Union* abounded in rumours; it was said they were bound for Ireland and the Cape of Good Hope. Meanwhile they stayed just where they were, in Falmouth harbour, till Henry could bear it no longer. On 7 August he set out to walk those twenty-five miles. 'The joy of my heart was very great. Every object around me called forth gratitude to God. Perhaps it was joy at the prospect of seeing Lydia – though I asked myself at the time whether, out of love to God, I was willing to turn back. I persuaded myself that I could.' He stayed that night at St Hilary and went next day to Marazion.

Lydia was not at home. 'So I walked out to meet her, and when I met her coming up the hill I was almost induced to believe her more interested in me than I had conceived.' It was a very exciting moment and he re-turned to St Hilary in high hopes of seeing her often, only to find a message from Falmouth that the fleet was about to sail. Greatly disappointed, he left at once by the mail coach.

This second sudden appearance, two weeks after the earlier one, set Lydia thinking hard. 'I was surprised again today by a visit from my friend Mr Martyn. I feel myself called to act decisively. O Lord, I am so weak that I would fain fly from this trial. Help me to know and do thy will; may we each be divinely influenced; may prin-ciple be victorious over feeling.'

Next morning the sailing orders were cancelled, so Henry set out on foot and walked eight miles through the rain before getting a horse. This time he went straight to Marazion. But again she was not at home and he had to go on to St Hilary without seeing her. 'I learnt from our servant that he had called this evening and left a message that he would be here tomorrow. My future happiness and his, the glory of God, the peace of my dear mother, all are concerned in what may pass tomorrow.'

Tomorrow came, Saturday, 10 August, the day neither of them would ever forget. At St Hilary Henry rose very early and was at once uneasy because the wind was blow-ing from the north. He had a dreadful feeling that the fleet would sail. At 7 a.m. he walked down to Marazion, but was so anxious about the fleet that even the prospect of meeting Lydia gave him little pleasure. They were together briefly before breakfast and planned to leave the house afterwards and walk along the coast. It had been fixed that he was to preach next day both at Marazion and St Hilary. Lydia's mother had breakfast with them. As it was the 10th day of the month it fell to him to read Psalm 10 at the end of the meal. Lydia then opened her Bible at Genesis chapter 10 and handed it to him. At that moment the door opened and a servant announced that the fleet was sailing. A horse had come for him from St Hilary where a carriage was standing by to rush him back to Falmouth. 'It came upon me like a thunderbolt.' And he saw that Lydia was dreadfully shocked too. 'She came out so that we might be alone at taking leave. I told her that, if it should appear to be God's will that I should be married, she must not be offended at receiving a letter from me. In the great hurry she revealed more of her mind than she intended. She made no objection whatever to coming out. Thinking perhaps that I wished to make an engagement with her, she said we had better go quite free. With this, I left her.'

He galloped to St Hilary. The signal gun had been fired at 5 a.m. It was nine o'clock when he left Lydia and noon before he got to Falmouth. For the moment the struggle to reach the ship drowned all other considerations. Most of the fleet had already put to sea but the anchor chains of *The Union* had fouled other lines, so the chaplain, of whom they had abandoned hope, scrambled on board, thanking God that the passage to India was not lost, and telling no-one where he had been.

They passed Lizard Point that night, and on Sunday morning, as Henry rose to preach on deck, they were in the middle of Mount's Bay and he could still see the spire of St Hilary's church. He and Lydia had had so little time to talk and plan, or even to understand one another.

Parting under such pressure, even her last remark was ambiguous. Towards evening he stood on the deck again, gloomy and sea-sick, unimpressed for once with the glories of sunset over the Atlantic, cut to the heart every moment by what had happened. And she, so near, was saying, 'My affections are engaged past recall', and then adding 'It is now clearly understood between us that he is free to marry where he is going and I shall often pray the Lord to find him a suitable partner' – which was not at all Henry's view of the matter.

6 I speak to stones

Out in the mists and raging storms of the Atlantic Ocean
the navies of England and France sailed and counter-
sailed in the maze of manoeuvres leading up to the
Battle of Trafalgar. Apart from one brief peace the war
had dragged on for thirteen years and there was still a
decade of war to come. Henry had lived with it since
he was a child, but now he was directly involved. *The
Union* carried the 59th Regiment, and in the convoy there
were fifty other transports, packed with 8,000 soldiers,
escorted by four warships and accompanied by some of
the great sailing vessels which regularly made the trip to
the East. Among all these, Henry was the only chaplain.

In those days there was no Suez Canal, so they went
first to Cork in Ireland, where the invasion threat held
them up for another two weeks, and then to Madeira
Island *en route* for Salvador in Brazil. By then they had
been three months out from Falmouth. Henry was fortu-
nate enough to have a cabin to himself, but he had no
really like-minded companion on this tedious, dangerous
voyage. So he had to learn a new independence, maintaining his Christian life and witness among men who
mostly regarded him as a mad enthusiast.

Sea-sickness and sorrow combined to torment Henry on
the five-day trip to Cork. He had left everything and lost
everybody. The reality of the step he had taken overwhelmed him. 'When we spoke with exultation of missions

49

to the heathen, what an imperfect idea did we form of the sufferings by which it must be accomplished.' But Cork proved a haven of peace. He had never been out of England before. He walked the eight miles into town and realized he was in a Roman Catholic country. Noticing a soldier sitting under the wall of the fort, he did not hesitate to argue against prayers to the Virgin Mary and all trust in our own good efforts. Delighted with the intelligence of the man's objections, he 'opened to him the system of the gospel'. This was his normal way. He did not shirk controversy or hesitate to risk giving offence by boldly declaring his message.

On board ship he read to a group of soldiers and their wives from *The Pilgrim's Progress*. This was only the first of many such readings from Christian books, which continued throughout the voyage and sometimes attracted large numbers. Distressed by the godlessness and profanity of the men, Henry distributed Bibles and tracts: 'The more I see of the world, the more deeply I am struck with the truth and excellence of the gospel. May these my poor, wretched countrymen who sail with me, whom I see under the power of Satan, be turned away from their sin to God.' The captain would allow one Sunday service, no more, so, as the only actively witnessing Christian on board, Henry adopted an aggressive policy, boldly going on to the lower decks to speak about Christ. 'Every oath they swore was a call on me to help them.' Some gave him a hearing; others deliberately turned their backs, or walked off, picking their way along the deck between the sleeping forms of those who had been on night watch.

Since all the ships were anchored together at Cork he took the opportunity to visit some of them. On one he found a court-martial in progress, following the discovery of a plot to murder the officers, so he returned to *The Union* 'as to a kind family of friends'. Next he tried a Botany Bay ship carrying women convicts to Australia.

The women thought he was a Catholic priest and the captain refused him permission to preach. 'I went away much shocked at the iniquitous state of this ship.' Back on shore he was confronted by the skeletons of two murderers, hanging in chains. 'It gave me a new idea of what sort of people God had to manage. With my face towards the wide and lovely ocean, I thought, thou hast sent me as a sheep among wolves, yet my heart too is the same, disposed to the same iniquities.'

From Cork they sailed into an Atlantic gale. Henry stood on deck 'in a sort of patient stupidity, very sick and cold' and could neither think nor sleep as the wind howled through the rigging and the ship heeled and tossed between towering waves. His porthole broke open and his cabin flooded. *The Union* dropped behind the convoy and was thus in danger of capture if a French raider appeared. But the gale raging in his heart was even harder to bear.

With better weather the chaplain revived. He began tutoring in mathematics and French, resumed his study of Urdu, moved around the ship talking freely about Christ, read books to those who felt inclined to listen and preached on Sundays, unless the captain cancelled the service. His preaching was not popular and the general opinion was that 'Mr Martyn sends us to hell every Sunday'. They acknowledged his sincerity but disapproved of his emphasis. Henry had a low opinion of himself as a corrupt sinner and regarded others in the same way. Chastising himself, he chastised them too, not hesitating to rebuke those who swore or got drunk, and warning everyone of death, judgment, and 'the threatenings of God', as well as telling of the possibility of new life in Christ.

The issue came to a head one Sunday in September. An officer told him, 'You must not damn us today or no-one will come again.' Henry felt most uneasy at the prospect of preaching but regarded it as his duty to put before them 'the truths which they hated'. All the officers sat behind him that day, so that if necessary they could walk out together. In the event only one did so, though Henry was unwise enough to speak from so provocative a text as 'The wicked shall be turned into hell and all the nations that forget God'. It was his impression that God had greatly helped him and that many of the men had been deeply moved, but when he went below decks to read to them that afternoon not one came.

Henry had no-one to advise him. His academic successes and linguistic gifts had concealed his immaturity and the limitations of his training. Indeed he had had no training at all to be an army chaplain and his bare fourteen months as Simeon's curate had not really been long enough to reshape his ardent and turbulent spirit. 'I feel my unfitness as a missionary. I don't shrink from any known method of diffusing the light of truth, but I am not ingenious, I do not invent ways and means of getting at men. Yet what can I do but preach, read to them as the business of the ship permits, and converse with whoever I can get to join me?'

It was Sunday, 29 September when they anchored at Funchal, capital of Madeira Island. The service on board was cancelled, so Henry went on shore, as he had the address of a Christian barber from London. Although he had conformed to the prevailing Catholicism, the man got Henry a room and meals. This was a great help, as the fleet bound for the West Indies was also in port and the two inns were crowded. For four days Henry lived on shore, talking about the Lord Jesus Christ to all he met and rebuking an American who saw no harm in drunkenness and thought all sincere people were equally good. There was such congestion in the little harbour, called upon to service 150 ships at once, that it took him hours to get back to *The Union*. He seized the chance of mailing a letter to Emma in Plymouth. 'God knows how dearly I love you and Lydia and Sally and all his saints in England, yet I bid you an everlasting farewell almost without a sigh.' At sunrise the East and West Indian fleets sailed together into the vast emptiness of the Atlantic.

It took them another forty days to reach Brazil. Henry continued his usual intensive programme of Bible study and prayer, meditation and Scripture-memorizing. Some words in Milner's *History of the Church of Christ* – 'To believe, to suffer, and to love was the primitive taste' – so gripped his mind that he thought no uninspired sentence had ever affected him as much. In that sense he longed to be 'a man of the ancient primitive simplicity'.

Apart from the weekly sermon he had to take the initiative in finding work for himself, and in this he was increasingly successful. A sergeant 'said with some emotion that many of the men were the better for my coming among them, and that he himself had been brought up in this persuasion and now things he had almost forgotten were being brought back to his mind'. A soldier who had been a choir-boy helped him start singing sessions 'and the men got round us in great numbers'. Their hardships exceeded his, as he realized when he took water to the sick, but found he could not read to them as lights were not allowed. A man named Mackenzie became increasingly friendly, read the Bible with him in his cabin, told him of the defects in his preaching and passed on the comment, 'Martyn is a good scholar but a poor orator.' This depressed him and, as the Battle of Trafalgar broke out away to the east of the convoy, Henry was wondering if he was really only fit to be a bookworm. 'I thought at night of living in a beautiful country united to Lydia – but I could see no pleasure in it. I have declared war against the world, the flesh, and the devil. My single enquiry shall be – what is the Lord's will? Thus, Christ strengthening me, I shall triumph in faith and be content with such gifts as I possess, and improve them.'

He used to sit with the Indian sailors on watch, try out his Urdu and struggle to understand their talk. He enjoyed their kindness and attention. 'These Muslims seem quite delighted if I speak to them and they are eager to help me out. They addressed me as I passed today. But though I can say a little to them, I cannot converse with them. My heart burns with desire to impart the gospel of God to them and I think with delight upon the day when I shall be able to speak fluently the precious truths of eternal life.' Meanwhile he had to learn 'to do the will of God where you are and leave the rest to him'.

Soon after crossing the Equator the whole fleet came in the night on to a line of reefs. Two ships were lost but thanks to prompt action by the look-out man *The Union* miraculously escaped. The coast of South America came in sight. As the fleet was running into Salvador, the old capital of Brazil, Henry got into a vehement dispute with an army captain in the saloon as a large number of soldiers looked on. The captain maintained that there was no harm in getting drunk, that the Bible was mostly priestcraft and that God was to blame for giving him the kind of nature he had, but 'he had nothing to say to which the Lord did not give me a ready answer'. Indeed it is probable that in debate the chaplain was more than a match for anyone on board.

Brazil was at that time a Portuguese colony. For sixteen days Henry broke away from everything English and gave himself delightedly to the country, the Brazilians, the negro slaves and the Portuguese. On disembarking on to the quay he sat down at once in a tiny negro shop. Large numbers of negroes crowded in, amazed at such friendliness in a European, 'very good-looking, cheerful people, all endeavouring to assist me in speaking the Portuguese words, the radical parts of which I knew from

the Latin. One woman asked, Are the English baptized?'
Then he walked through the town wondering 'when will
this beautiful country be delivered from idolatry and
spurious Christianity?' Out of curiosity he strolled into
the garden of a magnificent house. A young couple came
to find out who the intruder was. 'I spoke to them in
French and was very politely asked to sit down.' And thus
he fell in with Senhor and Senhora Antonio Corre, with
whom he spent much of the next two weeks.

Antonio, a graduate from a Portuguese University, was
delighted to meet someone from Cambridge. 'A slave
was sent to gather three roses for me.' They met daily and
Henry was shown the pepper and tapioca plantations, the
orange and lemon groves and the cultivation of coffee
and cotton. 'At Antonio's father's house I was described
to them as one who knew everything – Arabic, Persian,
Greek – and all stared at me as if I had dropped from the
skies. A priest came in, so I spoke to him in Latin. He
blushed and said he did not speak it. I was so sorry I had
unintentionally pained him. In my bedroom a slave
washed my feet. I was struck with the degree of abase-
ment expressed in the act. As he held my foot in the
towel, with his head bowed down towards it, I remembered the condescension of the blessed Lord. May I have
grace to follow such humility.'

Visiting churches together, Henry talked to Antonio
about worship and the Bible, but found his mind more
liberal than religious. 'I told him the English reformers
were led to prison and flames rather than conform to
idolatry. I also spoke about the new birth, but he did not
seem to pay much attention.' On the last day 'the slave
who had attended me burst into tears when I parted from
him and was going to kiss my feet. But I shook hands
with him, much affected by such extraordinary kindness
in people to whom I had been a total stranger a few days
before. Antonio and his wife came out to the garden gate

and continued looking till the winding of the road hid me from their sight.'

Along with this ability to win the affection of the uneducated and the respect of the learned, went Henry's remarkable boldness in controversy and witness. Seeing a friar 'I followed him through the cloisters and addressed him in Latin. He was a little surprised, but replied. I asked him to prove from Scripture the doctrine of purgatory, image worship, the supremacy of the pope, and transubstantiation. His arguments were exceedingly weak and the Lord furnished me with an answer to them all. Two more friars joined in. I confuted all their errors as plainly as possible from the Word of God. As we passed along the passage one of them asked me whether I was a Christian. We reached a cell and sat down. I asked for a Bible and the dispute was renewed. They appealed to the authority of the church and seemed most surprised at my knowledge of Scripture. When the sun set they all went with me through the long, dark passages. They were exceedingly polite and enquired when I was coming ashore again.' Henry asked one of them if he thought his life as a friar was according to the will of God. Though the man said he did not know, Henry was impressed by 'his tenderness, affection, and humility, so exactly resembling the true demeanour of saints'. While convinced that the principles on which his own life was built were better, Henry was left wondering whether his behaviour gave adequate proof of it.

Muslims singing their songs rowed him back to *The Union* as he talked with an Englishman who thought it enough to tell men to be sober and honest. 'And so in one hour I have seen the power of the devil in three forms, that of Popish and Muslim delusion and that of the natural man. I never felt so strongly what a nothing I am. All my clear arguments are useless; unless the Lord stretch out his hand, I speak to stones.'

7 The open, restless sea

Tormented by sickness on the ships and storms on the
sea, it took the convoy another five weeks to get from
Salvador to the Cape of Good Hope. Everyone was depressed, including Henry, who seemed to make little
progress with his work among the troops. Through the
tedious struggle he remembered Lydia and looked forward to seeing her in heaven. 'If we have lived and died
denying ourselves for God, triumphant and glorious will
our meeting be.'

Five men had the courage to associate openly with
him, though he could really rely only on Mackenzie and
Major Davidson. The Sunday sermons continued to be
an ordeal: 'There is scarcely one who encourages me by
an attentive hearing and none at all who strengthens my
hand by a kind word on the subject.' Davidson tried to
explain to him that his preaching was not calculated to
win the men, because 'I set the duties of religion in so
terrific a light that people were revolted. I felt the force of
his remarks and determined in future to make more use
of the love of God.' Together they read and discussed the
first five chapters of the Epistle to the Romans, sitting in
Henry's cabin. While Henry was delighted at his increasing understanding, such an intense session was perhaps
too much for the Major, who did not often come again.

The very sharp line Henry drew between sacred and
secular, the things of God and the things of the world,
separated him from the soldiers, preventing him from

entering into the normal interests of their lives. While his character and brilliance appealed so much to scholarly men, he was not well suited to be an army chaplain. Mackenzie did his best, admitting he had almost burst out in abuse of the preacher, but thankful that God had delivered him from this satanic temptation. 'He hoped I would go on preaching boldly, however offensive the truth might be.' When the ship's captain died at Christmas, Henry was with him to the end, reading the fifty-fifth chapter of Isaiah and the sixth chapter of John's Gospel. In response the captain whispered, 'Lord, evermore give us this bread.'

At the dawn of 1806 Africa was in sight and the fleet anchored north of Cape Town, near Robben Island. But the Cape meant war, for it was at that time a Dutch colony and had come into the conflict on Napoleon's side after he had overrun Holland. England had already conquered it once but now had to do so again to keep open the sea route to the East.

A beach-head was established, the 59th Regiment landed, and on 8 January the Battle of Blaauberg was fought. Nearly a thousand men lost their lives, mostly on the Dutch side. Henry was not allowed on shore till the fighting ceased. Then he succeeded in attaching himself to a stretcher party accompanied by a doctor, and walked for six miles towards Cape Town. On the top of a little hill they came across a British officer and his men, lying dead in the sunshine. 'I shuddered with horror at the sight.' They did what they could for the wounded: 'All whom we approached cried out instantly for water.'

On reaching the scene of the main engagement they found farm-houses converted into a hospital, where hundreds of men were lying in rows, covered in blood. Henry spent some time talking in French with a wounded Dutch officer. He then returned with the doctor to the battlefield, still strewn with dead and wounded. 'A Hottentot lay with extraordinary patience under his wound on the burning sand; I tried to make him comfortable and laid some bread near him.' Another wounded man was cursing the Dutch. 'I told him he should rather forgive them and begged him to pray to Jesus Christ.' The doctor went back for more equipment and Henry was talking in French to an injured Frenchman when suddenly a drunken Highlander appeared and asked him roughly, 'Who are you?' Henry said he was English, but the man raised his gun and shouted, 'No, no, you are French.' Fearing he might actually fire, Henry sprang up towards him, saying that if he doubted his word, he could take him prisoner to the camp.

Two days later the Dutch surrendered. 'Pleasing as was the cessation of warfare, I felt considerable pain at the enemy being obliged to give up everything to the victors. I hate the cruel pride that makes men boast over a conquered foe. I had rather be trampled upon than be the trampler.'

For a month Henry had lodgings in Cape Town, preaching often at the military hospital. But after his single-handed struggles with soldiers at sea, he was longing for personal friendship of a different kind. He hunted the town for eighty-year-old Dr Vanderkemp, agent of the London Missionary Society at the Cape, of whom he had read at Cambridge. 'At length I found him. He was standing outside the house, looking up at the stars, with a great number of black people sitting around. I introduced myself and he led me in and called for Mr Read. I was beyond measure delighted. Meeting these beloved brethren so filled me with joy and gratitude to God that I hardly knew what to do.' He revelled in their family worship, even though it was all in Dutch. Sitting in the open at night with Table Mountain before them he was thrilled with their account of the triumphs of the gospel in Africa. 'Talking with Read on the beach, we spoke of the excellency of missionary work. The last time I stood on the shore with a friend, speaking on the same subject, was with Lydia at Marazion, and I mentioned her to Read. However, I felt not the slightest desire for marriage and often thank God for keeping me single.' When Vanderkemp gave him a Syriac New Testament, Henry asked the old man if he had ever regretted being a missionary. 'No,' he said, smiling, 'I would not exchange my work for a kingdom.'

He devoted one day to climbing Table Mountain, thinking as he did so what uphill work the Christian life was. The many months his journey had already taken, and the vast distance traversed, brought home to him his friendless condition. Remembering those he had loved 'it seemed like a dream that I had actually undergone banishment from them for life'.

Ten weeks after leaving Table Bay they reached Madras. This final stage of the nine-and-a-half-month journey from Portsmouth was the most trying of all. Heavy seas, lack of sleep, increasing heat and inadequate food produced general bitterness, much illness, and led to some deaths. Though he filled his days with Bible reading, prayer, tutoring in maths and the study of Urdu and Persian, Henry's efforts to help the men were not much appreciated and he was 'ready to cry out, "What an unfortunate creature I am, the child of sorrow; from my infancy I have met with nothing but contradiction." ' In this mood he passed his twenty-fifth birthday on the open, restless ocean.

Braving the ridicule and abuse of others, Mackenzie came almost every night to Henry's cabin to study the Bible and pray, often staying for hours. 'I rejoiced to find so much of a Christian spirit in him. He was a great comfort and relief to me and we had much conversation about the temptations we are liable to and the strength which is to be found in Christ.' A drunken captain, seeing Mackenzie reading on deck, yelled at him, 'Damn the Bible.' He told Henry the officers were saying, 'Martyn will be sharing in the plunder of the natives of India and he doesn't care whether it's just or not.' This revived some of his own doubts about the lawfulness of receiving his salary from the East India Company. At heart he wanted no connection with it but – 'other thoughts have occurred to me. A man, who has unjustly got possession of an estate, hires me as a minister to preach to his servants. The money with which he pays me comes unjustly to him, but justly to me. The Company is the ruling power. If I were to refuse to go to India I might on the same grounds refuse to go to France, just because the monarch who pays me is not the lawful one.'

At last they sighted Ceylon and the very smell of land was reviving. But they lay becalmed in terrific heat. Henry was not sure he could endure it for long and suffered from some distressing shortness of breath: 'If I die, I die to be happy; if I live, I shall live to glorify God.' And as they moved northwards he prayed with new earnestness for the setting up of God's kingdom in India. He saw India for the first time on 21 April and next day they landed at Madras, where he found himself at once in the middle of an immense crowd. That night 'while turbaned Indians waited on us at dinner, I could not help feeling as if we had got into their places'.

As before, he found lodgings on shore and one night he persuaded his servant to take him out to his own village. 'Here all was Indian – no vestige of anything European. I walked by moonlight, reflecting on my mission and God wonderfully assisted me to trust him. What surprises me is the change of views I have here from what I had in England. There my heart expanded with hope and joy at the prospect of the speedy conversion of the heathen. But here the sight of the apparent impossibility requires a strong faith to support the spirits. Even if I never see an Indian converted, God may design by my continuance in the work to encourage future missionaries.'

On his first Sunday he preached at Fort St George before the Governor of Madras, who asked for a copy of the sermon, though most of the Europeans seem to have thought it too severe. Next day, in the presence of many others, the Port Admiral exclaimed, 'Upon my word, Mr Martyn, you gave us a good trimming yesterday', which so took Henry by surprise that he had nothing to say.

They sailed from Madras in dreadful heat. 'Exertion seemed like death, indeed absolutely impossible.' Reaching the Hooghly River on the western edge of the vast delta of the Ganges, they edged their way cautiously eighty miles upstream to Calcutta. On 16 May Henry went ashore at daylight and with some difficulty found William Carey.

8 The invitation to Lydia

After breakfast with Carey, Henry had a long dispute
about the gospel with an English-speaking Brahman. 'I
was really surprised at his acuteness and his acquaintance
with Scripture. He spoke with remarkable eloquence to
show that Christianity and Hinduism did not materially
differ and then asked me to explain my system and prove
it from the Bible.' Henry then travelled for ninety
minutes up the Hooghly River to Serampore, where he
was warmly welcomed by David Brown, an evangelical
Yorkshireman who had come twenty years before to run
an orphanage for the East India Company. Brown proved
a splendid friend to Henry and lodged him in a pagoda
at the riverside.

For the next five months Henry passed frequently between Calcutta and Serampore, seeing nothing else of
India. He continued his study of Urdu, often preached in
English and talked long with the outstanding group of
Christian men around him. There were ten Baptist
missionaries in Serampore, led by the famous trio, Carey,
Marshman and Ward. In Henry's view, 'three such men,
so suited to one another and to their work, are not to be
found in the whole world'.

His sermons in the Mission Church in Calcutta, where
the Governor-General, Sir George Barlow, was sometimes present, were so blunt and biblical that they
aroused the hostility of the resident chaplains. One

Sunday morning, before helping to administer the Lord's Supper, Henry had to sit through a sermon which was a direct attack on his own 'inconsistent, extravagant and absurd doctrines'. The preacher maintained that to say repentance was God's gift would encourage men to sit still and wait for God; to say human nature was wholly corrupt would induce despair; and to suppose Christ's righteousness sufficient to justify us would cause men to think it unnecessary to have any of their own. 'I started at hearing such downright heresy. He said I spoke only to gratify pride and uncharitableness.' This tension continued throughout his months in Calcutta, though David Brown had at first hoped he would settle there permanently.

He suffered other problems commoner among new arrivals. 'The constant uneasiness I am in from the bites of mosquitoes made me rather fretful.' A high fever alarmed the Browns, brought the doctor out in a hurry at night and distressed Henry by making study and writing impossible for days. He found that illness and heat increased his irritability, while the lack of expert help in learning Urdu made him feel he was losing ground in the language. And still he kept his harshest criticism for himself and was never satisfied with what he was or did. 'How easy it is to preach about Jesus Christ, and yet to preach oneself.'

Henry was an activist, itching to get at his life-work. 'I feel pressed in spirit to do something for God. Everybody here is diligent, employed in his proper work, but I am idle, tossed in uncertainty. I have hitherto lived to little purpose, more like a clod than a servant of God; now let me burn out for God.'

The friend God gave him at that moment was Dr Marshman, Carey's colleague, whose mind teemed with plans for the propagation of the gospel. At his home

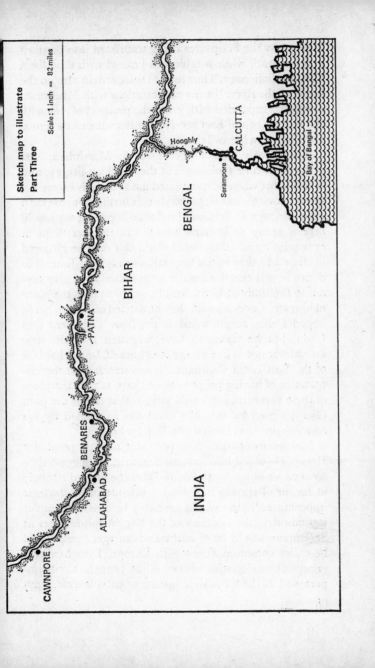

Sketch map to illustrate
Part Three

Scale: 1 inch = 82 miles

Bay of Bengal

CALCUTTA

Serampore

Hooghly

BENGAL

Ganges

BIHAR

PATNA

BENARES

ALLAHABAD

INDIA

CAWNPORE

Henry saw the Scriptures being translated into Sanskrit and Gujarati, while a table was littered with data for a Chinese dictionary. They used to walk arm in arm on the banks of the river. 'In my conversations with Marshman our hearts expanded with joy at the prospect of seeing all the nations of the East receive the doctrine of the cross. He is indeed a happy labourer.'

Henry took time to get used to Marshman, was grieved when he spoke against the Anglican liturgy, and 'a little hurt when he questioned me as though I were the merest novice – but he probably sees further into me than I see into myself'. At first Marshman hoped Henry would take a group of Indians inland and support them in evangelistic and educational work. But then he changed his tune and they had a long talk one night in June. 'His desire now is that I should stay at Serampore, give myself to the study of Urdu, and be ready to take the place of him and Carey, should they be carried off.' Marshman hoped Henry might translate the New Testament into Urdu, but he seems to have forgotten that the new arrival was not as free an agent as himself, but a chaplain of the East India Company. 'I was struck with the importance of having proper persons here to take the place of these two men, but could not see that it was the path God designed for me. My mind was so excited by the conversation that I could not sleep for hours.'

Marshman continued to pour out new proposals for Henry. He urged him to study Sanskrit. He suggested he went as a missionary to China. Then he argued strongly in favour of staying in Calcutta because of its strategic importance. 'Many would probably be converted under my ministry, the nearness of the Baptist missionaries at Serampore would be of mutual advantage, there would be easier communications with Europe, I might direct groups of missionaries who could be brought to Serampore and at the same time pursue oriental learning myself. Whereas if I went inland, he felt my usefulness would be limited to my own individual labours, it would be two years before I could be understood, and I would probably lose heart. I was much perplexed and so excited I could get little sleep.' Remembering Simeon's advice to break away from the company of Europeans, he was hoping he could get the East India Company to send him inland, either to Benares or to Patna. So many possibilities were bewildering. 'I have been running the hurried round of thought without God. May the Lord direct my way through this labyrinth.'

On Saturday, 12 July Henry went down river with David Brown and his family from Serampore to Calcutta and found there his first mail from England – letters from Simeon and Sargent, from Emma, Tom and Lydia. These were their second letters. All the first batch had been lost in a ship captured by the French. 'I longed to see Lydia's, but the one I did receive from her showed the extraordinary zeal and activity of her mind. Simeon's letter contained her praises too, and even he seemed to regret that I had gone without her.' So next morning he read her letter to Brown, who was delighted with it and urged him to get her out to India, saying it would be essential. They sat up far into the night discussing the matter. And so the issue of marriage was revived and much of his peace of mind removed in the process. He found it hard to concentrate on anything else for long. He could even say, 'Anxiety about the education and conversion of children rather terrifies me.' He talked it all over with Marshman too.

Then on 30 July he wrote to Lydia. 'At last I sit down to request you to come out to me to India. You are acquainted with much of the conflict I have undergone on your account. It has been greater than you or Emma have imagined. Your letter to me delighted Mr Brown and induced him to say you would be the greatest aid I could possibly meet with. My reason is fully convinced of the expediency – I almost said, the necessity – of having you with me. While it is possible that my reason may still be obscured by passion, let it suffice to say that now, with a clear conscience and the enjoyment of the divine presence, I calmly and deliberately make the proposal to you. If God shall forbid it I think, by his grace, I shall even then be contented.'

His high hopes ran away with him a little as he assured her, 'You will meet with no hardships. The voyage is very agreeable. The climate is fine. The dreaded heat is really nothing. The whole country is a land of peace and plenty, multitudes of simple people sitting in the shade listening to the words of eternal life.' Anticipating that she would get his letter at the end of the year, he advised her to catch the fleet sailing in February 1807. Her brother would make the arrangements. If Henry was away, David Brown would meet her, and she would come as a visitor to the Brown family. She should learn some Urdu on the voyage. And he ended by telling her, 'I have long loved you most affectionately. However, you shall decide, dearest Lydia, and we must not doubt that you will be divinely directed.'

It was March 1807 before she even received the letter.

Disturbed by the re-emergence of this matter, he found 'the agreeable female society I meet with in India very dangerous, producing a softness of mind and an indisposition to bold exertion'. He discovered his besetting sin was different from what he had supposed and of dreadful power. He experienced 'agonizing conflicts with my corrupt affections. Yet in the name of God I say that heaven and earth shall pass away before I will yield. The right hand shall be cut off and the right eye plucked out a thousand times, but the will of God shall be done.'

A month later he wrote to Lydia again, enclosing a copy of his earlier letter in case the original went astray. 'I sometimes regret that I did not obtain a promise from you to follow me at the time of our last parting. The instant your mind is made up, you must write. My dearest Lydia, I cannot say what I feel, I cannot pour out my soul, but I pray that you may love me, if it be the will of God.'

Temptation continued to buffet him. 'I can see no fit emblem of my soul but the burning bush.' And in September he had another letter from her – not, of course, an answer to his. He was transported with delight, 'though it may prove at last no more than a waking dream'. At once he replied. 'Till I am assured of the contrary I shall find pleasure in addressing you as my own. If you are not to be mine, you will pardon me. I am encouraged by the words you used when we parted, that I had better go out free, implying – I thought – that you would not be unwilling to follow me if I saw it to be the will of God to make the request. You will not suppose, my dear Lydia, that I mention these little things to influence your conduct, or to implicate you in an engagement. No, I acknowledge that you are perfectly free. Your heart is probably far less interested in this business than mine.'

And then his affairs moved forwards. He heard that he was definitely to go to Patna, and he welcomed to Calcutta his friend Daniel Corrie, another man moulded by Simeon and destined one day to be Bishop of Madras. They talked and prayed together, and travelled up the river to Serampore. Henry rejoiced to hear Corrie preach. 'God be praised for another noble witness to his truth.' The more he saw of idolatry in India the more he marvelled that so few of his friends came. 'Were not the zeal of our forefathers almost evaporated in these times, a body of learned young clergymen would come forth with joy to so glorious a work.'

On the morning of 15 October 1806, Corrie, Brown and Henry boarded a houseboat on the river, heading inland. As they passed the Baptist Mission, Marshman saw them. 'He could not help coming aboard. He dined with us and after going a little way left us with a prayer.' They moved slowly northwards into the vast interior of India.

Henry had exactly six years to live.

9 The disappearing chaplain

Corrie and Brown stayed two days on the boat with Henry and then he was alone with Indians for the first time for the six-week trip, north to the Ganges and westwards along it to Patna. To be towed upstream is, for the passenger, a most delightful form of travel. Cut off from the rest of the world, Henry studied Sanskrit, Arabic, Urdu, Persian, Greek and French, read the Koran and the Hindu epic, *Ramayana*, and studied his Bible. There was time to walk on shore, shoot birds to improve his diet, and talk about the gospel to those he met.

Women would flee at sight of the foreigner, but he went boldly into markets on the river bank, asked who could read, and gave out tracts and sometimes New Testaments. One evening, after the boat had tied up for the night, he found an old Brahman working in the fields, who told him with the utmost bitterness that the English had robbed the Indians of their country. Another man overheard this and felt he should make amends by referring to 'the brave English'. Henry spoke to them about the day of judgment, heaven and hell. They paid great attention, but he knew this was only because he was a foreigner and that probably they did not understand half of what he said.

In a host of such encounters as this he began to sense the feelings of the people. One day his stick happened to touch the brass pot in which the crew's rice was boiling. 'So defiled are we in their sight that the pollution passed from my hand, through the stick and the brass to the food, and they threw it all away.'

Studying and talking, watching and listening, he profited greatly from this experience of being alone in India. 'I learnt that the power of gentleness is irresistible and also that these men are not fools. Clearness of reasoning is not confined to Europe.' Troubled by his failure to convince his fellow-travellers of the validity of the gospel, he watched the river gliding by under the moon and reflected that in a few years there would be a new generation of Hindus, Muslims and English in the land, and God could raise up new and better witnesses than he.

Patna in Bihar was at that time the fifth largest city in India. Along with its small British satellites of Dinapore and Bankipore it stretched for fourteen miles along the Ganges. Henry lived in Dinapore with 400 British troops and forty-five officers under the command of General Clarke, who was kind to him and continually invited him to his bungalow for meals. However, Henry had so much enjoyed being alone with Indians on the river that he was not pleased to be back in the kind of situation he had faced on the voyage. On his first Sunday the General ordered his men to attend divine service. 'As there was no seat for anyone I was asked not to detain them by a sermon.' He tried to comfort himself playing the flute in his dreary rooms. 'I frittered away the morning by marrying a couple and calling on General Clarke to ask him to put a stop to games on Sunday.'

Although culture-shock had not been so named in his time, Henry was not the last missionary to find that his enthusiasm to bring the knowledge of Christ to Asians produced in him a strange hostility towards his own people. Yet he was lonely and would muse with painful joy on those he loved so much in Cornwall and Cambridge. The arrival of mail from Emma and Lydia at

Christmas was emotionally overwhelming. 'The torrent of vivid affection which passed through my heart continued for four hours.' He was a pioneer, belonging to no Mission, with no colleague to advise or correct him, and there was his relationship to Lydia to cope with as well. 'Lydia is a snare to me. My heart is still entangled with this idolatrous affection and consequently unhappy.' One night he saw her in his dreams. She had arrived in India, but as they talked he said to her, 'I know this is a dream. It is too soon after my letter for you to have come.' And so he woke. 'Perhaps all my hope about her is but a dream.'

There was frustration too in his Indian friendships. He found it hard to keep his temper with his Urdu teacher's 'Muslim bigotry'. Travelling into Patna he was conscious of being eyed with angry contempt. 'Here every man I meet is an enemy. Being an enemy to God he is an enemy to me. But he is an enemy too because I am an Englishman. What a wonderful place heaven must be, where there are none but friends. Indeed England appears almost a heaven upon earth, because there one is not viewed as an unjust intruder.'

Should he then have gone back where he belonged? Should all European Christians have kept out of countries dominated by their government's armies in the nineteenth century? Many have apparently thought so, blaming Christians for following the soldiers and getting involved in colonialism. But Henry, Simeon, Corrie-Brown and all that generation who believed in Jesus felt bound to obey his command to preach the gospel to every creature. Viewing his job in that light, Henry carried on. 'Though the heathen rage and the English people imagine a vain thing,' he wrote in parody of the second Psalm, 'the Lord Jesus, who controls all events, is my friend, my master, my God, my all. I continued writing till late at night, much impressed with the importance of my work and the wickedness of wasting a moment when so many nations are waiting till I do it.' It was true. They were.

But that work, in which he was much more interested than in British soldiers, was shrouded in complexity. He found that his Urdu was too refined to be understood by anyone except servants of the English. Then the Urdu of Bihar was different from that of Calcutta, and itself changed every few miles within Bihar. He dreamed of publishing the Gospels in the four main variants of Bihar Urdu, to be followed by Genesis, the Psalms and the Ten Commandments. The gifts of a chaplain to the armed forces he might not have, but he was one of the most talented Christian linguists there have ever been.

And so, in spite of everything, at the end of 1806, the seventh year of his life as a Christian, Henry could say that things had turned out better than he had expected. It was his guess that he did not have another seven years to live and this imparted to his life a single-minded intensity not very attractive to his fellow-countrymen.

Throughout 1807 Henry lived at Dinapore, fourteen miles from Patna. Although his first duty was to the British soldiers, he had only one Sunday service at which to preach. There was normally a good congregation of privates and the families of European business men; but few officers attended. Each week he also visited the hospital to read from *The Pilgrim's Progress* and other books, as he had done at sea. His only close British friends were Major and Mrs Young. Almost every week he had a meal at their home, rejoicing in their Christian faith, though he did not agree with some of the amusements Mrs Young thought allowable, and she felt that he dwelt too much on the negative side of the gospel. Once when they suggested that the congregation had enjoyed his sermon, 'I told them I was not pleased to hear it. Unless their hearts are pricked it would be better I had never preached.'

The Youngs were invaluable to him because they were on the spot, but he was closer in spirit to Corrie, who stayed with him on the way to his post 150 miles further inland. They wrote to each other every fortnight and then, at Henry's request, increased this to once a week. It became his regular Monday morning task. When an answer from England took eighteen months it was priceless to have 'such a friend and brother in the kingdom of Christ stationed so near me'. There was not a single Indian Christian in Patna. Among the British officers Major Young was the only one to declare himself a Christian, but there was a group of soldiers who came twice a week to his room to read the Bible, sing and pray. 'To escape as much as possible the taunts of their wicked companions they go out of their barracks in opposite directions to get to me.'

Many of the soldiers had taken Indian women, so sometimes Henry was asked to conduct weddings and baptisms. Occasionally he refused to baptize women who showed no sign of faith and repentance, even if this caused great distress. One of the weddings took place on his own twenty-sixth birthday, and in order to conduct it Henry travelled 100 miles up the Ganges, taking seventeen hours each way. The journey was considered so dangerous that he made his will before starting out. As he saw the couple's happiness he marvelled that these things seemed to go so easily for others, yet with such difficulty for him. On the way back he saw a bearded, white-haired Brahman sitting under a large tree by a pagoda, and garlanded with flowers. The man was singing in Sanskrit and expounding the Hindu classics to an attentive crowd. 'I waited for the first pause to ask some questions, which led to a long conversation, and ended by my attempting to give them a history of redemption.'

75

In Henry the chaplain was for ever disappearing into the missionary.

Another wedding trip took eight days, for two of which his boat was aground on a sandbank in a hot hurricane of suffocating dust. Though this did not stop him studying and translating the Scripture into Urdu, he confessed, 'I could scarcely keep myself alive and was much tried by evil temper.'

One day, 'The thought suddenly struck me how easy it would be to translate the church service into Urdu for the soldiers' wives and women and children.' In a few weeks the job was finished and on Sunday, 15 March, he conducted Sunday worship in Urdu for two hundred women, many of them Muslims or Catholics, and preached in the language for the first time.

Numbers were not always so high, and he was never sure how much they understood, but he kept at this task every week from then on. The women thought it a great honour to come to church and wondered why he took so much trouble over them. The limitations of his own Urdu distressed him and he feared his constant use of the same words must prove tedious, but these unfortunate people, camp followers of the British Army, fell naturally into his sphere as chaplain and were part of his steadily expanding circle of action.

So were the three schools he started at his own expense among Indian children. After the first rush to get in, panic spread when it was rumoured he intended to turn all the children into Christians, set a mark on the best of them, and whisk them away to England. But he was wisely slow to introduce Christian books, and the teachers, who were not Christians, calmed the fears of parents. On Henry's first visit to the Patna school, a crowd quickly gathered. 'I told them it was not my intention to make the children Christians as they understood it – that is, to leave caste and be baptized – but to make them good men.' Even General Clarke had a look at the school and was impressed, but told Henry, 'You will make no proselytes.' Some local schoolmasters resented the competition of free schools backed by a foreigner. In at least one case Henry paid a man a salary till he found another job.

Yet neither the soldiers, nor the women's meeting, nor the schools had first place in his heart. That was reserved for Bible translation, for which many-headed linguistic research was a delightful essential, daily involving him in debate with his assistants, one a Hindu, one a Muslim. In this realm he was intellectually stretched to the utmost, absorbing the languages, culture and religions of the country at break-neck speed. This was just as well, for time was not included among the many gifts God gave to Henry Martyn. Weakened by overpowering heat and by bouts of illness, frustrated and opposed throughout the year, he was driven forwards by his God-given genius for languages. Though his basic task was to translate the New Testament from Greek into Urdu, he also extended his knowledge of Hebrew and gave time to Persian, telling David Brown as early as May that 'the Persian New Testament appears to me of incalculable importance, as the language is spoken all the way from here to Damascus'. This extra load, instead of crushing him, was intoxicating, suggesting vast new areas of outreach for Christ.

As his helpers talked and disputed with him, Henry began to understand the way Asians thought about Christianity in those early days of missionary approach to the vast continent. At that era the gospel was totally identified with the invading, imperialist, immoral European. Only that year Robert Morrison, the first Protestant missionary to China, got a foothold on the mainland, but there was not yet a single evangelical Chinese believer. Nor was there one Christian among the millions of Javanese. Only Europeans claimed to be Christians, and the vast majority of them were ignorant of the faith and denied it by their behaviour. The English, who had robbed India of her freedom, were the Christians. So Henry's helpers assured him that not only were Christians regarded with hatred and contempt, but that the first Patna people to become Christians would undoubtedly be murdered. While they gave Henry the respect due to the conquering race, the more familiar they became with him the more violently they attacked what he held most dear.

They considered the New Testament to be filled with blasphemies. After translating the First Epistle of John, Henry asked the Muslim what he thought now about the deity of Christ and the Trinity. 'He said he would never believe it, because the Koran had declared it sinful to say God had a son. The very terms "Father" and "Son" were degrading. I explained that God was not literally Father and Son as these terms are used among men, but names used by God as the nearest to explain the relationship between these two persons. I advised him to pray that God would teach him what the truth really was. He said there was no need to pray on this subject, as the Word of God was clear. I asked him whether some doubt ought not to arise in his mind whether the Koran was the Word of God. At that he grew angry. I would have done better to leave the words of the chapter with him without saying anything.'

When Henry stated that until our hearts are changed we are abominable in the sight of God and that our works, however useful to men, are worthless before him, his helper became furiously angry and said he had a question to ask: 'What would become of children if the disposition they were born with rendered them odious in the sight of God? I gave him the best answer I could. He considered it as nothing because it was founded on the Bible. With great contempt he said it was all a matter of faith – the same as when the Hindus believed the nonsense in their books.' He insisted that the incarnation was not necessary – 'if we had all perished God would not have suffered loss.' Forgiveness presented no problem to him: 'I pardon my servant very easily, and there's an end of it.' And then, 'How do you know the Jews did not alter the Old Testament? They were wicked enough to do it.' Though the Hindu assistant was less aggressive, he was just as ready to degrade the name of Jesus. None of the Hindu gods was 'so low as to be born of a woman; every sect wanted to exalt its teacher, so the Christians did Jesus'.

These debates hit and hurt Henry. Anti-Christian ideas clamoured for control in his own heart. He found relief in writing to Corrie, 'My tongue is parched and my hand trembles from the violent onslaughts I have had this day. Ever since I declared the way of Christ, the serpent has thrown off his mask.' The Muslim said one day, with dreadful bitterness, that 'after the present generation has passed away a set of fools would perhaps be born – such as the gospel required – who would believe that God was man and man God'. He objected that there were no difficulties in Christianity, it was a life of carelessness – devotion only once a week, prayers when and where you like, eating with or without washing. And he thought himself perfectly righteous, assuring Henry he had never committed any sin in thought, word or deed. 'I told him he was very far from the kingdom of heaven, which he did not like.'

So Henry came to know what Christianity had to contend with in knocking at the gates of India. Yet he remained thrilled with his superhuman task. 'It is delightful to see the truths of the Epistle to the Romans in their Urdu dress. Never did I see such wisdom and love in the

New Testament as since I have been obliged to study every expression, never did I realize the beauty of the language and the importance of the thoughts as I do now. Though in a manner buried from the world, I rejoice that I am not yet twenty-seven years old and, unless God orders it otherwise, I may double the number in constant and successful labour. If not, God has many more instruments at his command and I shall not cease from happiness by departing into another world. What shall separate us from the love of Christ? Neither death nor life, I am persuaded. May it please God to make bare his arm in this country, as aforetime in Greece and Rome, and plant some churches in the land.'

10 Not Lydia but Sabat

England seemed to have vanished: mail was so rare, so late. But in July Henry had a letter from Lydia, still written before she had received his from Calcutta. He would have liked to see a stronger expression of her love. 'In the evening I sat for a long time at my door after the great fatigue of the day to let my mind relax, and found a melancholy pleasure in looking back upon the time spent at St Hilary and Marazion. How the days and years are gone by, as a tale that is told.'

At the end of the month he heard from her again, and there were also letters from Simeon, Sally and Laura. Laura was twenty-eight and married. She told Henry that she was dying. Sally wrote again a few weeks later to say that she had been to see Laura just before the end: she had truly turned to Christ, and there had been a remarkable change in her at the last. For one day Henry suspended all translation work. 'My heart was choked at the remembrance of my sister. How great has been the mercy of God to my family in saving us all. How dreadful would be the separation of relatives in death, were it not for Jesus.'

A still greater shock came on 24 October. 'I received at last a letter from Lydia in which she refuses to come because her mother will not consent to it.' From Lydia's point of view, 'The pain of writing to him is over and I feel satisfied I wrote what duty required.' None of her letters to him has survived, but we have all of his letters to her.

He at once wrote a very long one, reviewing every aspect of their relationship. 'My heart is bursting with grief and disappointment, my dear Lydia, but I do not write to blame you. Permit me to reply calmly to your letter of March 5th, which I have this day received.' He gently directed a battery of arguments at Mrs Grenfell, even suggesting she should come to India too, and optimistically promising not to try to persuade Lydia to leave her. Fastening upon an apparent loophole in Lydia's letter, which stated that present circumstances prevented her coming, he suggested they should get engaged – 'My own heart is engaged, I believe, indissolubly, but until your answer arrives I must endure another eighteen months of torturing suspense.' So they were still left gazing towards one another across the vast spaces of the world.

Unknown to Henry a valiant attempt had already been made to turn the matter in his favour. Learning that she had refused to go, and somewhat regretting his previous advice to Henry in favour of celibacy, Simeon travelled all the way to Cornwall, while Henry was enduring that hot hurricane on the sandbank in the Ganges. He called at the Grenfell home in Marazion and met Lydia for the first time. Mrs Grenfell agreed that Lydia should go with him to Major Sandys' home in Helston, where they had a long talk. 'She stated to me all the obstacles to Henry's proposals. First, her health; second, the indelicacy of her going out to India alone on such an errand; third, her former engagement to another person – it had been broken off and he had gone to London two years ago to be married to another woman, but as he was still unmarried it seemed an obstacle in her mind; fourthly, the certainty that her mother would never consent to it. On these points I observed that I thought the last was the only one that was insurmountable.'

The best he could do was to extract from Lydia a promise that if her mother said she did not want to stand in her way they would take this as God's guidance and she would inform Simeon. However, he saw little chance of it, and in fact Lydia did not communicate with him again. His visit was 'a cordial to my fainting heart and I enjoyed seeing how a Christian lives', but her hesitations were not removed. Only a few days later she heard that Corrie's sister was going to India to visit her brother, and she distressed herself with the thought that Mary Corrie 'may be the partner appointed for my dear friend'. Yet she did not go herself.

Mrs Grenfell's opposition to the match was broadly based. The rest of the family was married and Lydia was living with her in the old home. Lydia's father does not appear normally to have been part of the household. She said dissension was the family's besetting sin. It often raged: parents against children, brother against brother, sister against sister. In addition to this domestic distress, which made even rational discussion difficult, Mrs Grenfell did not share the evangelical faith to which, like Emma, Lydia clung. One day 'I conversed with my dear mother on the sinfulness of our hearts and our need of Christ. I was enabled to speak faithfully on the dangerous state all were in who trusted in anything but Jesus Christ and to tell her plainly that she was trusting in herself and her works, not in Christ, who – if the Bible was true – was the only way to God. Though for the present she seemed to laugh at all I said, yet she was not angry.' So Mrs Grenfell had never been enthusiastic about this friendship with ardent Henry. She also knew that his family had inherited poor health from their mother and that Laura, only in her twenties, was at that moment dying. To go to the ends of the earth during a major war in order to marry a diseased person of fanatical faith did not seem to her sane. And she had already witnessed the unreliability of Lydia's affections in the breaking of her former engagement, about which she had so guardedly spoken to Simeon. Yet it remains surprising that she could prevail over a daughter aged thirty-two.

Why then did Lydia allow herself to be held back? The arguments about health and indelicacy could hardly be taken seriously. And Simeon, the resolute bachelor, had little sympathy for her point about the former engagement. But that actually lay closer to the root of the problem than did Mrs Grenfell's opposition. It was not until her twenty-seventh birthday on 19 October 1801 that Lydia began to keep a journal. Unfortunately it was not a diary of facts and events, but just a record of her inner and spiritual thoughts. By then her engagement to Samuel John of Penzance had been broken for more than a year. Whatever happened to part them took place on 23 June 1800. It was in 1800 that Lydia came to a knowledge of Christ as her personal Saviour, but this does not seem to have caused the breach. Indeed, in June 1802 she referred to the rift between them as 'the great transgression of my life. O what a week was this two years ago. What mischief did one false step lead me into. I hate and abhor myself for my conduct towards a tender friend. Yet I will hope for pardon, even for the sins of departure from God and broken vows to man. I found my soul enlarged to pray for him, and something like hope arose in my bosom, at least a willingness to wait in dependence on God. I feel guilty and my sad conduct two years ago often weighs down my spirit. I am separated from him on earth, perhaps for ever, yet my heart is more closely united to him than to any earthly object. God knows the truth of all I say. When I sleep it is he that engrosses my last thoughts. The idol is not destroyed and I lament that

84

still my heart is given too much to him.' A few weeks later she 'enjoyed three hours of serious converse with H.M.'. This is her first reference to Henry, but she had no special feelings for him at that time.

Then in February 1804, just before Henry came seriously into her life, and almost four years after parting with Samuel, she heard that the latter was to marry. While this distressed her, she was thankful it freed her from fear of his death, by which she had long been haunted. So she felt she could 'drink this cup with a smile of gratitude to God. I now resolve to resist the temptation to employ my thoughts on one whom I must cease to love, or I should be guilty of sin. Bless him, Lord, and give him a blessing in her he has chosen. My heart says, Bless them.' Years afterwards she cut out the next four lines in her journal.

Yet Samuel was still not married when Henry's letter came. In fact he remained single till January 1810. Right up to then she thought of him as the person she had injured and deduced 'I am not free to marry'. She regretted having made the mistake of giving Henry some encouragement at the time when she understood Samuel was on the verge of matrimony. By 2 March 1807, when Henry's Calcutta letter arrived, she had for almost seven years become accustomed to living with a hopeless love, the lover gone far away to London, and never likely to appear again. She could muse on him tragically, with a certain wistful comfort. Then Henry was substituted for Samuel, but in the same situation, even further away in India, probably never to return. And again she could muse on him tragically, with a certain wistful comfort. She had got used to that.

What held her back then, her mother or the still celibate Samuel John? It was a combination of the two, but chiefly the long, broken relationship with Samuel which deprived her of the will-power to respond to Henry by actually going to India. She never made the slightest attempt to do so. After all, she was a village girl from the remote end of England, and had never contacted the wider world, as he had done at Cambridge. Yet she did not quite say No to him. She kept him as her hopeless love. 'It is my duty to familiarize my mind with the idea of our separation being for ever. I feel as if he was the inhabitant of another world. In heaven we shall surely meet and in perfect holiness and joy for ever live together.'

But Henry needed escape from hopeless love. It is true that at times even he had misgivings. Once, when he felt sure she would come, he confessed, 'I felt miserable at the prospect of marriage, because I must bid adieu to that sweet freedom from care with which I am now blessed, and the problem of the education of children made me greatly fear marriage.' But her refusal shattered such doubts. Without Lydia he saw no point in his new house and garden. He told David Brown to auction the attractive set of china that was coming to him. And Lydia need not have worried about Mary Corrie. Henry certainly didn't. He remained totally faithful to his first love, his only love.

Instead of Lydia, Sabat arrived. He came two weeks after her letter, surviving the danger of assassination on the way from Calcutta. For Sabat was an Arab who had become a Christian. As Muslims, he and his friend Abdullah had visited Mecca and then gone to Afghanistan, where an Armenian lent Abdullah an Arabic Bible. He became a Christian and fled for his life to Bukhara in Russia. There Sabat met him again, denounced him, and witnessed his martyrdom. Sabat then wandered to India, where he too fell in with a copy of the Arabic New Testament, compared it with the Koran, and turned to Christ. In 1804, when he was twenty-seven, he was baptized in

Madras. His brother, sent from Arabia to kill him, succeeded in wounding him with a dagger. Sabat then devoted himself to propagating the gospel and joined the translation staff at Serampore, giving good service on the Persian and Arabic Scriptures. When the Baptist missionaries there decided to commit to Henry the translation of the New Testament not only into Urdu, but also into Persian, they sent Sabat to him, along with his wife, who was pregnant.

Their first day together was eventful. As it was Sunday, Henry preached to the Europeans. Sabat went along too, but, while Henry was in the vestry, an Indian claimed for some European the chair on which Sabat was sitting. He rose in great anger and stalked out. Afterwards he admitted to Henry that he had two natures, his old one, which was a soldier's and sometimes got the better of him, and the Christian one.

That night Sabat dined with Henry at Major Young's and joined the six soldiers who came to pray. He had his own bungalow but worked and ate with Henry. 'The very first day we began to spar. He would come into none of my plans, nor did I approve of his.' But they also prayed, and their lives were so interlocked that they influenced each other. 'Sabat has filled me with ideas of going to preach in Arabia or Persia, so that I begin to wish Lydia may never come – but this is the thought of a day.'

Sabat told Henry tearfully about the sin he still found in himself. 'If the Spirit of God is given to believers in Christ, why am I like this after believing for three years? Every day I determine to keep Christ crucified in my sight, but I forget to think of him. I rejoice when I remember God's love in Christ, but I am like a sheep, feeding happily while he looks at the grass – but when he looks behind and sees the lion, he can't eat.' Henry assured him his experience was that of all the children of

God, even of Paul, and suggested they should keep together. 'If it please the Lord to call me to labour in the gospel with him in Persia, we might encourage one another to be faithful unto death, ready to lay down our lives for the Lord Jesus.'

It was Sabat who turned his thoughts to Persia, a radical idea for a chaplain of the East India Company already involved in Bible translation into Urdu. 'Sabat's conversation stirs up in me a great desire to go to Persia, as by his account all the Muslim countries are ripe for throwing off the delusion. He and I agree better in the faith of Christ than in anything else. He looks down with high contempt on European learning and civilization. This nettles me to take up the cudgels sometimes, but his ignorance of English scientific terms and my ignorance of Persian are a most happy gag to our mouths.'

And the new friendship saved him from much brooding on what might have been.

11 Mirza and Sabat

Soon after Sabat had joined him, a Muslim named Mirza
Fitrut arrived from Benares to work with Henry on the
Urdu New Testament. On the first day they sat together
for three hours discussing Christianity and Islam. 'He
said there was no passage in the Gospels which said that
no prophet would come after Christ. I showed him the
last verses in Matthew, the passages in Isaiah and Daniel
on the eternity of Christ's kingdom, and proved it too
from the nature of the way of salvation. I then told him
my objections to Islam: its laws, its defects, its un-
necessariness, the unsuitability of its rewards, and its utter
want of proof. When he mentioned Muhammad's
miracles I showed him the sixth and thirteenth chapters
of the Koran, where Muhammad disavows such power.
Nothing surprised him so much as these. Poor man, he
said I had produced great doubts in his mind. Having
spent his youth in useless poetry he now wishes to pass his
declining days in the study of Scripture.'

Henry liked Mirza. They had many arguments as they
worked together, but these were always conducted in a
quiet, friendly manner. 'In translating 1 Timothy 1:15
I said to him, "You have heard the gospel in that verse;
your blood will not be required at my hands; you will
certainly remember these words at the last day".' Mirza
acknowledged this, but the doctrine of the Trinity remained a problem to him. 'If I take clay and mould it,' he
said, 'it can have no comprehension what I am. How

then should we know what God is?' Once he challenged Henry, 'Sir, why don't you try to save me?' to which Henry answered, 'I would lay down my life to save your soul.'

They worked together happily, though Henry complained that Mirza was too pliable, prone to give in, 'like a ball of wax, easily moulded into any shape'. But as time went on, friction increased between Mirza and Sabat. There were faults on both sides. Sabat was jealous and easily angered. Mirza deliberately vexed him and told lies to discredit him, and Henry was caught in their crossfire.

Eventually Sabat so hated Mirza that he never spoke of him except with contempt. 'He stoutly maintains his superiority to Mirza in Urdu, which is utterly ridiculous. He is angry with me for not hating Mirza too, according to the Arabian proverb that a friend is an enemy to his friend's enemy. But in this work of translation Mirza is invaluable because of his knowledge of English. May the Lord long preserve him.' Eventually the incessant insults drove Mirza to Patna. In a month he returned to Dinapore, but a week later was compelled to resign altogether from the translation work. Henry pursued him to Patna and endeavoured to smooth matters out, at least till the four Urdu Gospels were finished; but in vain. 'My greatest trial is Sabat. He spreads desolation here. Mirza is driven to Patna and he himself talks every day of going, saying he cannot live with these wicked Indian people. He little thinks his own wicked heart is the cause of all his troubles. And he still holds fast the diabolical doctrine that love of our enemies is not necessary. Last night I preached on humility and angered him much, as he said I intended it for him, but that if he knew more English he could preach infinitely better.'

Only Henry's exceptional Christian forbearance and devotion to duty prevented a similar breach between himself and Sabat, whose behaviour as they worked together on the Persian New Testament was often intensely provocative. 'He is much given to contradicting and setting people right. He looks on the missionaries at Serampore as so far below him in intellect that he could write on a text so deeply that none of them would be able to follow him. He is certainly versed in the learning of the Arabs but I wish it could be made to sit a little easier on him. I look forward to reaching Paul's Epistles in hope that some good will come to him from them. He seems to think himself infallible. If in our disputes I get the better of him, he is stung to the quick and does not forget it for days. So I avoid as much as possible all questions gendering strife. But if he sees anything wrong in me, any appearance of pride, he tells me of it without ceremony, and thus he is a friend indeed. He describes so well the character of a missionary that I mean to sell my great house and take the smallest quarters I can find.'

But worse was to come. 'Sabat fell into one of his furious passions, thirsting for revenge on a servant who had offended him. The man sent word he would not return. Sabat fetched his sword and dagger. With lips trembling with rage he vowed he would kill the man if he did not come, and then sell his life dearly by killing every policeman or soldier sent to apprehend him. I argued for a long time and prevailed so far as to get the weapons away from him. He told me I must bring none of the Word of God near him as his conscience was telling him he was disinclined to obey it.'

Month after month this struggle continued. 'Sabat has been tolerably quiet this week, but think of the keeper of a lunatic and you see me. He supposes he is so under the influence of the Holy Spirit that there will not be a single error in the whole Persian translation. He looks upon Europeans as mushrooms and seems to regard my pretensions to any learning as we do those of a savage or an ape. I am much tried by his horrible temper, but my God and Saviour continues to support and strengthen me.'

Somehow the translation progressed and there was some visible answer to Henry's prayers. 'He is increasingly dear to me as I see more of the meekness and gentleness of Christ in him. Our conflicts are over, I hope, and we shall draw quietly together. We have laboured hard today, from six in the morning till four in the afternoon. He is certainly wonderfully improved and has resolved never to strike a servant. A few days ago he did give an unfortunate blow but his conscience smote him immediately; he fell upon the man, kissed his hands, asked pardon, and gave him money.' When the Persian New Testament was at last finished it was Sabat who proposed they should kneel down and give thanks to God. 'He is very dear to me. I cannot help considering it one of the most interesting events of my life that I became acquainted with him.'

Then there was another explosion. Sabat quarrelled with his Indian landlord, so he and his wife went round the garden and tore up every shrub, plant and flower in it. 'All these evils spring from nothing but horrible pride and this makes me fear for his soul. How such a temper can be consistent with a state of grace I am at a loss to conceive. He is universally detested by everyone, Indian or English, and is at this moment in great wrath walking to Patna.' Next day Henry escorted Sabat's wife to Patna and from then on he was constantly going there, fourteen miles away, to continue improving the Persian translation. 'I lament to see how little of his time is given to the work. Though I am there merely to collaborate with him, he will not stir beyond one chapter, however short, though it is done in an hour or two.'

During the whole of 1808 and up to his departure from Dinapore in April 1809 Henry heard only twice from

Lydia. It might have been kinder if she had not written at all. 'I received a letter from Lydia today which renewed my pain, though it contained nothing but what I expected. Prayer was my only relief and I found peace by casting my care on God. My mind was somewhat sorrowful that I was not to see her again till after death.' When the second letter came, 'I trembled at the handwriting, but it was only more last words sent on the advice of Major Sandys in case the previous letter had not arrived.' He had a feeling that before very long he would go the way Laura had gone. 'I had a dream last night which much affected me. I was walking down the street in Truro and about to enter my father's house, when a lion at the door prevented me.'

Meanwhile the Youngs were transferred elsewhere and so he lost the closest friends he ever made in the army. He had subconsciously enjoyed talking to Mrs Young without being too much attracted to her. Another unnamed couple took their place in his life to some extent, till they too were moved away. 'I could not help loving her as a sister, and to be separated from them was as painful to me as Mrs Young's departure. It seems a very peculiar providence that I never met such ladies in England. The families I have most loved in India have been very soon taken from me, leaving me deprived of something necessary to my happiness.'

Daily he toiled at improving the Persian New Testament with Sabat and translating the Urdu New Testament with Mirza. For relaxation he studied Persian poetry with the latter and the Koran in Arabic with the former. 'You will perceive that I am obliged to fag as hard as we ever did for our degrees at Cambridge.' Around his main tasks he wedged all manner of studies which kept his mind alert. On one day he speaks of reading a book in defence of Roman Catholicism, finishing Boswell's *The Life of Johnson*, studying the Koran, and translating a passage of the Bible into seven other languages. He resumed Arabic, read Aristotle and Aeschylus in the original, and also Sadi, the thirteenth-century Persian poet of Shiraz. He was then 'seized with a sudden desire to read Hebrew, chiefly to see language in its purest and simplest state, for it is my belief that language is from God. I remember one night I did not sleep a wink. One discovery succeeded another in Hebrew, Arabic and Greek, so rapidly that I was almost in ecstasy. My thirst after knowledge is very strong, but I pray continually that the Spirit of God may hold the reins.'

This thirst and this gift were harnessed to the task of revising the already completed Urdu New Testament. He drew in five learned Muslims from Delhi and Patna, a poet from Lucknow, and a descendant of the royal house of Persia. 'Almost every sentence was altered. I was amazed that they referred to the Persian in order to understand the Urdu, but it was a consolation to find that from the Persian they caught the meaning instantly, expressing their admiration for the plainness of the translation.'

12 Fighting the four-faced devil

With the arrival at Dinapore of the 67th Regiment, nine hundred of whose men proved to be Roman Catholics, Henry's position was transformed. There were some very large Sunday morning services and for the first time he really seemed to get his message across to the men. With the coming of summer, sickness became rife. 'The heat here is terrible and the nights almost insupportable. My employment is now very great every day. Sick and dying people have to be visited. I scarcely have time to write my journal. Many at the hospital require my attendance daily. The hospital is a town in itself. How shall I ever be faithful to them all?'

Instead of a few valiant men daring to make their way to the chaplain's house, a large group came each night. 'Several days this week my men were forty, and promising too, so that they are a great comfort to me. My spirit has been refreshed by ministering to them.' But there was some dissatisfaction: he was accused of preaching faith without works and of making little sins as bad as big ones. When one of his critics lost his temper and bayoneted another soldier, Henry blamed himself for not taking disciplinary action against him earlier. But at the end of his time at Dinapore he could say, 'My men seem to be in a more flourishing state than they have ever been. I hope they will prove to be true soldiers of Christ. Seldom, even at Cambridge, have I been so pleased.'

Meanwhile his health was steadily deteriorating. On 17 January 1808 'I found a pain in my chest for the first time, a consequence of over-speaking.' After one Sunday's work in March he was 'without strength or spirits for anything. I had better take warning in time before I am put upon the shelf.' But the trend continued, specially on Sundays when he had to preach to the soldiers, at the hospital, to the women and again at night. To David Brown in Calcutta he confided 'My poor weak body has been reminding me of its decay today. I am apt to be troubled with shortness of breath. Next rainy season I must climb some hill and live there. But the Lord is our rock. While there is work which we must do, we shall live.'

In September he became really ill. 'I just had time to finish the tenth chapter of Luke with Sabat and was then attacked by fever. What may be the issue God knows. Into thy hands, O Lord, I commit myself. Lord Jesus, receive my spirit.' He came through all right, cancelling engagements 'because of the weak and sore state of my lungs'. As he lay in bed, one of the soldiers came to read to him. 'Thus even in this life I have found sons and brothers according to the promise of the Lord. Yet I look back at times with fond regret to England and contrast the fresh, bracing air of my native land with the stagnant atmosphere of this sickening climate. I scarcely believe it possible I shall live through another rainy season.'

In October he spent a week convalescing in a river-boat on the Ganges, happy to have 'a friend in heaven who can never be unkind', but depressed about himself and introspective as he had not been for a long time. He tried to pray for the villagers he saw working in the fields. Yet it seemed futile to do so, as they could not possibly arrive at Christian faith since 'there was no Word of God to put into their hands and no preachers'. He told Sally his Sunday duties so exhausted him that he seldom recovered till Tuesday. 'The danger is from the lungs, though none of you seems to realize it.' Early in 1809 he felt he must stop the meeting for the women, which had continued for a year, but with decreasing attendance. Tuberculosis was steadily undermining his strength.

A handsome, young Italian monk came to minister to the Roman Catholics in the 67th Regiment – a Jesuit named Julius Caesar, complete with skull-cap, satin robes and rosary of costly stones. Though General Clarke threatened to tie him up and have him flogged if he came to the barracks again, Henry took a liking to him. One night Julius dined with him and they talked for four hours. Henry always regarded it as his duty to God to tackle awkward issues openly and bear witness to the truth. 'I told him I had some questions to ask about the Roman church. The first was about the adoration of the Virgin and the saints. I solemnly charged him and his church with the sin of idolatry. He answered in the usual manner, but not ably. The excesses he had seen at Geneva seemed to fill him with horror at Protestantism. He lifted up his hands and prayed earnestly that God would not allow him to be converted by me, nor let the Protestant religion come into Italy. The more I observe of his disposition, the more I like him. He is a serious, unassuming young man.' But their friendship did not deter Henry from reporting to Corrie, 'I feel my spirit roused to preach against popery with all the zeal of Luther. There are four types of people in India: the heathen, the Muslims, the Papists, and the infidels. You and I are sent to fight this four-faced devil and by the help of the Lord Jesus, whom we serve, we will.'

Julius was greatly agitated by their long talk. 'He could do nothing but walk about that night, but looked up to God and became tranquil.' He told Henry that if he had said such things in Italy he would have been burned. Further talks followed, stimulating Henry to learn Italian. And the presence of Julius encouraged some of the Catholic soldiers so that one day at the hospital a man spoke heatedly against Henry as a separator from the church. 'I rejoiced much and talked loud so that many might hear. The dispute lasted so long that men gathered from all parts of the hospital. I rose up and harangued with great liberty, testifying to my desire to learn the truth and my willingness to follow it. They would not take anything from my Bible, which they said was corrupted. I challenged them to produce a single text from their own to prove the adoration of the Virgin or the supremacy of the Bishop of Rome.'

An Armenian Catholic priest also came on the scene. 'I am almost ashamed of my appearance before such a venerable and appropriate figure. He kept my tongue employed all day. I tried him on spiritual things, but there he had nothing to say. Poor padre! With an exterior so imposing you would think St Peter was present, he knows nothing at all. Alas, how fallen from what their fathers were. When will the churches of Asia recover their ancient glory?'

In those days Henry had no closer friend than Corrie, who came again with his sister, Mary, and brought the good news that Thomason, Henry's fellow-curate under Simeon, had arrived in Calcutta with his family. Henry was beginning to look in the opposite direction: 'My purpose of emigrating to the west is not altered.' The west meant Persia. 'How interesting are the politics of the present day. Every event is like turning over a new leaf in a book of mysteries. Wars and rumours of wars reach my ears. I met a Christian from Aleppo and talked to him in Arabic. It gave me hope that one day I should be able to preach the gospel all the way from Calcutta round about unto Damascus.' But in spite of that he was rather abruptly ordered to transfer to Cawnpore. So ended two and a half years at Dinapore. Apart from Cambridge it was the longest stay he ever had anywhere.

Shortly before he left, the 53rd Regiment, also heading for Cawnpore, passed by. Its paymaster was a Christian named Sherwood, whose wife was destined to become well known as the author of stories about India. So for the only time in his life Henry was seen by a skilful writer whose eye observed details he himself never thought worth recording. As soon as their boat tied up, Mr Sherwood went off and found Henry 'in his church-like abode with little furniture, rooms wide and high, and many vast doorways and long verandahs'. In the evening they walked back to the boat together and Mrs Sherwood had her first sight of him. 'He was dressed in white and looked very pale, though that was nothing unusual in India. His light brown hair was raised from his forehead, which was a remarkably fine one.' She thought him not good-looking, yet found his face exceedingly impressive, 'so luminous, so intellectual, so affectionate – and there was a very decided air of the gentleman about Mr Martyn, and a perfection of manners which seemed almost inconsistent with the general bent of his thoughts to the most serious subjects. He was as remarkable for ease as for cheerfulness. In these respects his journal does not give a graphic account of him.'

Glad to get off the river, the Sherwoods spent two nights at Henry's home, 'which was destitute of every comfort, though he had multitudes of people about him'. Morning and evening there was family prayers with Bible reading and explanation. She saw that he was never drawn away from the prevailing purpose of his life, yet 'when he relaxed from his labours in the presence of his friends it was to play and laugh like an innocent, happy child – especially if children were present to play and laugh with him'.

13 Soldiers, languages and beggars

'I transported myself with such rapidity to this place,'
said Henry of his journey to Cawnpore, 'that I nearly
transported myself out of this world.' It was the hottest
time of the year. He could have got permission to post-
pone his trip or gone by boat, as Sabat did, but instead he
went by night in a covered litter, carried by bearers. But
beyond Allahabad he travelled for forty-eight hours, day
and night, without stopping, 'the hot winds blowing like
fire from a furnace'. He collapsed the moment he entered
the Sherwoods' bungalow on 3 May, and stayed there
ten days with fever and chest pains. When they remon-
strated with him for risking his life he pleaded his anxiety
to get on with the translation work. Unfortunately this
was but the first of a series of desperate overland journeys,
from which probably only a wife could have preserved
him.

The coolest place in the Sherwoods' house was the hall,
where he lay on a couch for two days 'with many books
near to his hand and amongst these always a Hebrew
Bible and a Greek New Testament'. A little Indian or-
phan girl used to draw her chair up to him and show him
the Bible verses she was learning. As he got stronger, 'He
sang a great deal, for he had an uncommonly fine voice.'
And right away a group of believing soldiers found him
out and came with Bibles wrapped in handkerchiefs. Mrs
Sherwood was delighted to hear them singing and praying together, but astonished at his artlessness when he

later sent a man to draw his considerable salary and bring it to him in cash.

Once he recovered, his life at Cawnpore followed the same general routine as at Patna. As chaplain, he was responsible for the spiritual welfare of the 53rd Regiment, the 8th Light Dragoons and six companies of Artillery. He pressed on with the study of many languages and with translation into Urdu, Persian and Arabic. And he again started schools for the poor. He did not shirk testimony and controversy with all he met. He continued to correspond with Corrie and Brown and occasionally letters came from far-away England. Twice a week he rode over for supper with the Sherwoods, which did much to preserve his health and satisfy his need for some family life.

Before sunrise on 15 May the soldiers of the 53rd had their first chance to hear the new chaplain. He faced a thousand men, drawn up in a hollow square. Even at that hour some of them fainted from the heat, but not Henry. A week later, though tormented by cold sweats at night, followed by fever and headaches all day, he preached to five hundred of the Light Dragoons lined up in the smelly riding school. The General in command was never very cordial to Henry and a private talk they had did not improve relations. 'While we were walking up and down I reproved him for swearing. Though it was done in the gentlest way, he did not seem to like it. I suppose it was the first time he had been called to order for some years. "So you are giving me a lecture", he said, and went on in an angry, confused manner to defend the practice of swearing.' Once again Henry had given a purely negative impression. Yet he worked hard for the soldiers, on one occasion, after a murder on the road, travelling under armed escort to Lucknow to marry a couple, and spending three whole weeks on another wedding trip.

It was the translation work with Sabat that really stimulated his talents. 'Sabat's behaviour has been exceptional. He is gentle and almost as diligent as I could wish. Everything seems to please him. His bungalow adjoins mine and is very neat, so from morning to night we work together. He much improves in his prayers and I hope he begins to see that, like the rest of us, he knows little or nothing.'

Mrs Sherwood also observed Sabat. 'Every feature in the large disc of his face was exaggerated. His eyebrows were arched, black and strongly pencilled. His eyes were dark and round, flashing with unsubdued emotion, ready to kindle into flame on the most trifling occasion. His nose was high, his mouth wide, his teeth large, his complexion bronzed, his beard and moustache black. He generally wore a silk jacket with long sleeves, loose trousers, an embroidered skull-cap with flaps hanging over each ear, earrings, shoes turned up at the toes, and a golden chain. A true son of the desert, he never sat on a chair without contriving to tuck up his legs under him. He spoke only Persian and Arabic, with a little bad Urdu, but what was wanting in his words was more than made up by the loudness with which he uttered them, for he had a voice like rolling thunder. Ameena, a very pretty young woman, was his seventh wife and she hated him most cordially. She was a Muslim and he was very anxious to make her a Christian. "Where do Christians go after death?" she asked him.

"To heaven, to their Saviour," he replied.

"And where do Muslims go?"

"To hell and the devil," answered the Arab.

"So you, being a Christian, will go to heaven?"

"Certainly."

"Then I shall continue to be a Muslim, as I would prefer hell and the devil without you to heaven itself if you were there." '

Yet Henry's extraordinary patience achieved a reasonably good relationship with his remarkable helper. 'Sabat is now happy for the first time in his life, and I must confess he does a great deal to make me happy. If wrath rises, he goes and prays and soon returns with a smiling face and a quiet heart. We are left entirely to ourselves in perfect solitude.' In this spirit of cordiality Henry, Sabat, the Sherwoods and sixteen soldiers took Holy Communion together one Sunday. At other times he was tormented by Sabat's laziness and by misgivings about the quality of his Persian. But Sabat would have none of it. 'I did not come from Persia to India to learn Persian.' And they went ahead with their translation of the Arabic New Testament, for Henry was convinced that the existing one was 'indescribably bad, not a translation but a paraphrase, and always wrong'. The very thought of a satisfactory New Testament in Arabic thrilled him. 'We will now begin to preach to Arabia, Syria, Persia, India, Tartary, China, half of Africa, all the south coast of the Mediterranean, and Turkey, and one tongue shall suffice for them all.'

Then Mirza Fitrut offered to join forces with him again on revising the Urdu New Testament, provided Sabat was not around. It is not clear how Henry kept the peace between the two men, but he came, to Henry's delight, and so Henry was involved in all three languages at once.

As though this were not enough, his linguistic gift continued to break out in all directions. For much of 1809 he kept his journal in Latin and Greek. 'After reading the Greek New Testament I feel a great desire to express myself in prayer in Greek and often do so. Also, after reading the Hebrew Bible I almost invariably express myself in Hebrew. I don't find that praying in another language diverts my attention much.' He was increasingly fascinated by Hebrew. 'My speculations occupy me night and day; they are always in my mind. I think when the construction of Hebrew is fully understood, all the scholars in the world will turn to it with avidity in order to understand other languages. I am continually speculating on it and on the nature of language in general.'

So he wrote to Brown for 'grammars and dictionaries of all the languages of the earth – do not stare, Sir, I have no ambition to become a linguist, but they will help me in some enquiries I am making.' Having listed seventeen languages, he specifically asked for data on Turkish, Hungarian, Armenian and Icelandic. Although such riotous visions kept the chaplain to the 53rd Regiment awake at night, he confessed, 'I would rather have the smallest portion of love and humility than the knowledge of an archangel. The conviction of my own ignorance is gaining upon me so fast that I have become a sceptic on all subjects except the Word of God.'

At times his sedentary life troubled him. 'What will friends at home think of Martyn and Corrie? They went out full of zeal, but what are they doing? Where are their converts? They talked of preaching under the banjan tree but now they seem to prefer a snug bungalow. I fear I should look silly if I went home now, chiefly because I should not be able to make people understand the state of things. If you itinerate like a European you will only frighten the people. If you travel like an Indian would, you will be dead in a year. Yet, as I write, hope and joy spring up in my mind. One day the Ganges shall roll through tracts adorned with Christian churches, cultivated by Christian farmers. All things work together to bring on that day. My part, to translate the Word of God, though not at first exactly according to my wishes, is appointed to me by God and is of more lasting benefit than my preaching would be. Besides that, I am sorry to say that my strength for preaching has almost gone.'

In spite of that, he did preach at sunrise on Sunday, 19 November 1809 to the Light Dragoons and again at noon at army headquarters. In the afternoon a letter came from Simeon telling him that Sally was dying of pulmonary tuberculosis. She was twenty-seven. He started to write to her, but a still more alarming letter from her husband showed him that it was no use. He guessed that she must already be with Christ. 'How soon shall I follow? I know it must be soon. Death is settled in my lungs.'

At the year's end the beggars came, huge crowds of them, and Sabat said, 'Why don't you preach to them? It's your duty.' He shrank from it. 'My carnal spirit says that I have preached for a long time to my servants without success and what can I expect from the very dregs of the people? But the true cause of my reluctance is shame. I am afraid of exposing myself to the contempt of Sabat and others by attempting to speak in a language which I don't speak well. However, I deserve contempt. I must get to the kingdom through great contempt. I must be pleased to be the filth of the world and the offscouring of all things. I will glory in my infirmities that the power of Christ may rest upon me.'

So on Sunday, 17 December he faced 400 beggars. 'I felt as if I were being led to execution. I told them I gave them with pleasure the alms I could afford, but I wished to give them something better too, eternal riches, the knowledge of God, which was to be had from God's Word. Then, producing an Urdu translation of Genesis, I read the first verse and explained it.' He had to go very slowly, as after each sentence there were interruptions, explanations and applause.

The following evening he attended a dinner party of army officers and their ladies. 'The splendour of these occasions does not dazzle me, as it once did. It appeared ridiculous and childish. I was sorry I had gone and thought I would rather be preaching to my beggars.

Looking along the crowded table, I could not with the utmost stretch of charity believe they were serious. They stayed dancing till early morning but I escaped immediately after dinner.'

The following Sunday there were 500 beggars and all he said was received with great applause. On the last day of the year even more came. Still on the first chapter of Genesis, he boldly asserted that the Ganges had been created by God and was not to be worshipped. 'I did not succeed as well as before, perhaps because I had more confidence in myself and less in the Lord.'

Mrs Sherwood often attended these meetings. 'No visions excited by the delirium of a raging fever can surpass the reality. They are old and young, male and female, bloated and wizened, tall and short, athletic and feeble, some in rags, some plastered with mud and cow dung, some with matted locks streaming to their heels, some bald, some with lips blackened with tobacco or blood-red henna juice. One man comes in a bullock cart, his head so large, his body so shrivelled, that he looks like a gigantic frog; another has his arm fixed above his head, the nail of the thumb piercing the palm of his hand; another has his ribs and face-bones traced with chalk, which makes him look like a moving skeleton.' Henry always shared in giving each person his copper at the end and would then lie down on his sofa, 'for he often said he had a slow inflammation burning in his lungs and he was usually in pain after speaking'.

14 Death in the lungs: visions in the mind

Henry remained in Cawnpore a year and five months, preaching to the beggars and the Europeans each Sunday and toiling at the translation work all week with Sabat and Mirza. 'Old Mirza gives me more satisfaction than anyone. He seems to take great pleasure in seeing an intricate sentence of the Epistles unravelled.' They completed the revision of the Urdu New Testament, though Henry was well aware that absolute excellence was unlikely to be achieved in these first efforts.

From Simeon he heard of Sally's death. 'She was my dear counsellor and guide for a long time in the Christian way. What is there now in this howling wilderness to charm me? I have no relation left to whom I feel bound by ties of Christian fellowship and I am resolved to form no new connections of a worldly nature.' Lydia, however, wrote to sympathize with him and suggested she might take the place of the sister he had lost. So he began a new series of letters to her. This may not have been fair on Lydia's part or good for Henry. For two and a half years, since she refused to come to him, he had turned aside from thoughts of marriage and been absorbed in his translations. Now the issue was reopened, and although Lydia might just regard him as an absent brother, it was not possible for him to treat her simply as a sister. Yet he was delighted to be in touch once more with 'my long-lost Lydia'.

And almost at once his health took a marked turn for the worse. It began on Sunday, 8 April 1810 after he had preached four times. All that week he had pain in the chest and lungs. The four meetings on the next Sunday completely laid him low and every conversation began to hurt him. He felt he ought to tell Brown. 'These symptoms are alarming in such a consumptive constitution as mine. Yet, why should I say alarming if, in the will of God, my time has come? Pray for me. Prayer lengthened Hezekiah's life; perhaps it may mine.'

He told Lydia, 'our family complaint has again made its appearance in me with more unpleasant symptoms than ever. Study never makes me ill, scarcely ever fatigues me, but death is seated in my lungs. It is speaking that kills me. May it give life to others. The call of Jesus Christ bids me cry aloud, so how can I be silent?' He promised to be careful and then included in his letter the gentlest of rebukes. 'Had I been favoured with the one I wanted, I might not now have had occasion to mourn. You smile at my allusion, at least I hope so, for I am hardly in earnest. I have long since ceased to repine at the decree that keeps us as far asunder as the east is from the west, and yet I am far from regretting that I ever knew you. The remembrance of you has kept me from many a snare. How wise and good is our God in all his dealings with his children. Had I yielded to the suggestions of flesh and blood and remained in England, I should without doubt have sunk with my sisters into an early grave. Whereas here, to say the least, I may live a few years to accomplish a very important work.'

He reduced his speaking engagements from four to two, but baptisms and funerals more than made up for this. 'I have not strength to do half my work.' Then one evening, while riding at full gallop, his saddle slipped and he was violently thrown. However, even in his weakness,

Henry was remarkably tough and the accident troubled him little.

Soon after Corrie and his sister, Mary, arrived on their way to Agra, the weather became unbearably hot. 'I scarcely knew how to keep myself alive.' Corrie took over some of his duties and this was such a relief that Henry persuaded the General to detain him in Cawnpore. For the next four months they worked together very happily. 'Corrie lives with me and Miss Corrie with the Sherwoods. We usually rise at daybreak and breakfast at six. Then we pray together, after which I translate into Arabic with Sabat. We dine at twelve and sit talking a little about our dear friends in England. In the afternoon I translate with Mirza into Urdu and at sunset we ride or drive and then meet at the church to raise our song of praise with as much joy, through the grace and presence of our Lord, as you do in England. At ten we are all asleep. Thus we go on. To the hardships of missionaries we are strangers.'

Lydia was a little anxious about Mary Corrie, but Henry quickly reassured her. 'You thought it possible your letter might find me married, or about to be so. Let me begin with assuring you, with more truth than Gehazi did his master, "Thy servant went no whither." My heart has not strayed from Marazion, or wherever you are. Five long years have passed and I am still faithful. Though you are not so usefully employed as you might be in India, I contemplate with delight your exertions at the other end of the world.'

But her letters had reawakened something in Henry which had lain dormant through the past years. One night 'I was walking with Lydia. We were both much affected and speaking on the things dearest to us. I awoke – and, behold, it was a dream. My mind remained solemn and pensive and I shed some tears. The clock struck three and the moon was riding near her highest noon. All was silence and I thought with some pain of the 16,000 miles between us – but good is the will of the Lord if I see her no more.'

Meanwhile he and Sabat made great progress with the Arabic New Testament. 'We shall never find in India so good a man as Sabat.' Yet Sabat's inaccuracies, even in copying out an agreed translation, were a constant torment to him: 'It is incredible the trouble I have to get anything correct, but all labour in the glorious cause is delightful.' In June he suggested to Brown that he should take this new Arabic New Testament to Arabia for improvement, 'having under the other arm the Persian to be examined at Shiraz. By the time they are both ready I shall have nearly finished my seven years and may go on furlough. If my life is spared there is no reason why the Arabic should not be done in Arabia and the Persian in Persia, as well as the Indian in India.' This was the seed-thought for the final period of Henry's service for the spread of the gospel in Asia. 'Thus it seems a new turn is given to my life. I commit myself confidently to God my Saviour. I know in whom I have believed and am persuaded that he is able to keep that which I have committed unto him.'

In Calcutta there was great satisfaction over the Urdu New Testament, high hopes for the Arabic, but no good opinion of the Persian, which was considered too full of Arabic idiom and too difficult for most readers. So Brown was not altogether hostile to Henry's new idea. 'But can I bring myself to cut the string and let you go?' he wrote. 'I confess I could not if you were strong and likely to last for half a century. But since you burn with the intense and rapid blaze of heated phosphorus, why should we not make the most of you? Your flame may last as long, perhaps longer, in Arabia than in India.'

Sunday, 30 September 1810 was his last working day

in Cawnpore. Corrie preached for him in the early morning. Then came the opening of the new church, whose building he had supervised. Corrie was in charge, Henry preached, and the regimental band led the singing. The place was crowded and the effort exhausted Henry so much that, on reaching his bungalow, he had to lie down on the sofa in the hall. The Sherwoods, Corrie and Mary were with him. They sang the hymn 'O God our help in ages past' and had lunch together. In the evening they all came again to hear his last address to the beggars. Strangely enough this was the only occasion on which he left the Old Testament to speak to them directly of the life and death of Christ, exhorting them to believe in him. Again he was worn out at the end, telling Mrs Sherwood, 'He was afraid he had not been the means of doing the smallest good to any of the strange people whom he had so often addressed.'

However, he was not altogether right about that. It appears that a group of educated young men had been present at one of the earlier meetings with the beggars. Out of curiosity they elbowed their way through the crowd and stood in a row with folded arms before Henry as he preached. One of them, a teacher of Persian and Arabic, was attracted by the novelty of the message. He avoided personal contact with Henry but persuaded Sabat to employ him in copying out the Gospels in Persian. When the time came to take the complete Persian New Testament to be bound in book form, it was entrusted to him. This enabled him to retain it long enough to read it all through. As a result, he came to faith in Christ and was baptized. He was eventually ordained in Calcutta Cathedral as a minister of the gospel, serving faithfully until his death sixteen years later.

On the morning of 1 October, Henry moved his possessions on to the boats in which he and Sabat were to travel down river. They did not sail till after dark, so he had time for a last ride, on which he caught sight of Mrs Sherwood. 'He accompanied me home and once again we all supped together and united in a last hymn. We were all low, very low.' They knew they would never see him again.

Though a cold wind blew through Henry's boat and bed that night, leaving him with pain in the chest, the journey to Calcutta, which took the whole month of October, proved a pleasant experience. They stopped for a day at Allahabad, Benares and Patna; he preached sometimes on shore, baptized a few children, and even conducted another marriage. But for the most part he was alone with his prayers, his books, his temptations and his high hopes for the future. After four years up country it was exciting to be near Calcutta once again. He turned out of the Ganges into the Hooghly 'with something of those sensations with which I should come in sight of the white cliffs of England'. And there was time to write at leisure to Lydia. In one of her letters she had suggested it might become his duty to return home. 'You ought to have added that, if I do come, you will consider it your duty not to let me come away again without you. But I am not likely to put you to the trial. I have just left Cawnpore to be silent for six months. I have no cough, nor any sign of consumption, except that preaching or a cold brings on pain in the chest, so I have been advised to rest. I have come forth with my face towards Calcutta, with an ulterior view to the sea.'

At sunset on the last day of the month he reached the Browns' home at Serampore and was overwhelmed by the welcome he received, 'children jumping, shouting, and convoying me in troops to the house. They are a lovely family and I don't know when I have felt so delighted as at family worship that night.'

15 The ruins of selfishness

For ten weeks Henry moved between Calcutta and
Serampore, as he had done four years before, making
arrangements to leave for Arabia and Persia. He was
with Marshman again, and the Youngs from Dinapore.
Thomason rejoiced to see him once more and promptly
sent off his impressions to Simeon. 'He is on his way to
Arabia in pursuit of health and knowledge. You know his
genius and what gigantic strides he takes in everything.
He has some great plan in his mind. As I understand it,
it is far too grand for one short life and much beyond his
feeble, exhausted frame. Feeble it is indeed – how fallen
and changed. Let us hope the sea air may revive him. In
all other respects he is exactly the same as he was. He
shines in all the dignity of love and seems to carry about
him such a heavenly majesty as impresses the mind beyond description. But if he talks much, though in a low
voice, he sinks, and you are reminded that he is dust and
ashes.'

At the close of the year he had his portrait painted, and
he preached before Lord Minto, the new Governor-
General of India, boldly taking as his text the story of
Paul before Felix. Later he dined with Minto and, in an
interview with him and the Commander-in-Chief, revealed his plans for Arabia and Persia. They raised no
objection, so 'I considered their compliance as indicative
of the will of God. I now pass from India to Arabia, not
knowing what things shall befall me there, but assured

that an ever-faithful God and Saviour will be with me. May he guide and protect me and bring me again to my delightful work in India. It would be a painful thought to suppose I would return no more.'

It was not easy to find a ship. One captain refused to take him in case he caused a mutiny by trying to convert the Arab sailors. However, Mountstuart Elphinstone, formerly Ambassador in Kabul, was travelling to Bombay and Henry was given a passage with him. He preached his last sermon on 6 January on the text 'One thing is needful' and next morning, 'without taking leave of my too dear friends in Calcutta', he slipped away.

For the next six weeks Henry's constant companion was Elphinstone, a very distinguished Scotsman, later Governor of Bombay, who was twice invited to be Governor-General of India, and twice refused. Henry greatly enjoyed his kindliness, classical education and wide knowledge of India. The respect was mutual and Elphinstone reported, 'We have in Mr Martyn an excellent scholar and one of the mildest, cheerfulest, and most pleasant men I ever saw. He is extremely religious and disputes with the Abyssinian captain about the faith, but he talks on all subjects, sacred and profane, and makes others laugh as heartily as he could if he were an unbeliever. He has proved a far better companion than I reckoned on, though my expectations were high. His zeal is not troublesome; he does not press disputes or investigate creeds. He is a man of good sense and taste, simple in his manners and character, and cheerful in his conversation.' Imperfectly though Henry may have communicated to most soldiers, he usually appealed well to those leaders of society whose paths he crossed.

In the Bay of Bengal the sea was very rough and Henry was sea-sick most of the time, unable to preach on Sundays, unable to think coherently, and consequently depressed. He lay on his bunk trying to conceive of perfect happiness. 'I find it impossible to create a terrestrial paradise, even in imagination. After trying this and that I see that there is enjoyment rather in giving than in receiving, in denying oneself for the good of others rather than in having a great number of good things for oneself. It is a greater happiness to obey God than to please self. Solid bliss is built on the ruins of selfishness. When I think of marrying I can reconcile myself to it more easily from considering it might add to the happiness of another than from the hope of gaining anything for myself.'

They stopped for a day at Colombo and walked together in the cinnamon gardens among the huts of the people along the shore. He cut off a piece of cinnamon bark to send to Lydia. Their Sinhalese guide spoke English. Elphinstone asked him about Buddhism in Ceylon but the man said he was a Christian. 'My heart bounded at hearing this. I got nearer and questioned him about the faith, but he did not seem to know much or to have felt as I hoped he had.'

Beyond Ceylon the weather was kinder and Henry successfully proposed prayers in the lounge every night for the Europeans, 'who, I am happy to say, are not averse to religious instruction. As for the Asians, they are as far removed from us in language, customs and religion as if they were inhabitants of another planet. Sometimes I speak a little Arabic to the sailors, but their contempt for the gospel and attachment to Islam make their conversion appear impossible.'

Rounding the tip of India he watched Cape Comorin. 'The waves seemed to wash the foot of the mountain, but as we drew nearer little churches were seen, apparently on the beach.' This reminded him of another beach and he sat down to write to Lydia. 'You do not tell me whether you ever walk there and imagine the waves that break at your feet to have made their way from India.

But why should I wish to know? Had I observed silence on that day I should have spared you much trouble and myself much pain. Yet I am far from regretting that I spoke. So seldom seeing a creature that cares for me, and never one that at all depends upon me, I begin to look upon men with reciprocal apathy. This sometimes calls itself "deadness to the world" but I much fear it is deadness of heart. I am exempt from worldly cares myself and therefore do not feel for others. Having got out of the stream into still water I go round and round in my own little circle.' It was a long letter, his first to her for three months, a sharing of thought and work rather than an outpouring of affection.

They stopped again at Goa, the Portuguese capital in India. Henry was very disappointed. 'I expected to find men, bishops and archbishops, learned friars and scowling inquisitors, but we were shown churches and monasteries, whereas I wanted to contemplate man, almost the only thing on earth which possesses any interest for me.'

On 18 February 1811, his thirtieth birthday, they reached Bombay. 'I am now at the age when the Saviour began his ministry, when John the Baptist called a nation to repentance. Let me now think for myself and act with energy. Hitherto I have made my youth and insignificance an excuse for sloth and imbecility. Now let me have a character and act boldly for God.'

His base for the next five weeks was Government House in Bombay. He was in the garden, reading mail from Calcutta, when the Governor himself appeared, 'So I told him all we had been doing and all we intended.' Thanks to his friendship with Elphinstone he was quickly introduced to other important people, including Sir James Mackintosh, who 'observed that the successors of Alexander the Great had made the oriental world Greek to make way for the religion of Christ and he thought the world would soon be Europeanized in order that the gospel might spread all over it.'

Mackintosh found Henry 'a mild and benevolent enthusiast, the sort of character with which I am always half in love, a man of acuteness and learning, though his meekness is excessive and he gives a disagreeable impression of effort to conceal the passions of human nature.' But on closer acquaintance he declared, 'Martyn, the saint, dined here; it was a very much more pleasant evening than usual; we had three hours' good discussion on grammar and metaphysics.'

More directly useful to Henry was his encounter with Sir John Malcolm who had spent a year in Persia negotiating political and commercial treaties on behalf of the British Government. 'Malcolm has given me letters of introduction to great men at Bushire, Shiraz and Isfahan, and also questions about which he wants further information. Perhaps I shall be taken up and hanged as a spy!'

A letter Malcolm wrote ahead to Sir Gore Ouseley, the British Ambassador in Persia, was to prove of great importance in Henry's career. 'I warned Martyn not to move from Bushire without your sanction. His intention is to go via Shiraz and Isfahan to Baghdad to try to discover ancient copies of the Gospels, which he and others are persuaded lie hidden in the mountains of Persia. His knowledge of Arabic is superior to that of any Englishman in India. He is altogether a very learned and cheerful man, but a great enthusiast in his holy calling. He has assured me, and asked me to mention it to you, that he has no thought of preaching to the Persians or of entering into any theological controversies. He means to confine himself to a search for old Gospels and giving a correct version of the Scriptures in Arabic and Persian. I told him I thought you would require him to act with great caution and not allow his zeal to run away with him. He declares he will not, and I must believe him. I am

117

satisfied that if you ever see him you will be pleased with him. His good sense and great learning will delight you, while his constant cheerfulness will add to the hilarity of your party.'

Sir Gore was indeed to be pleased with him, but the notion that he had no thought of preaching to the Persians or indulging in theological controversy was far from the truth. Just as Paul in his later years found himself taken away from Christian colleagues to associate with Roman soldiers and public figures who did not share his faith, so it was with Henry. Sally and Simeon, Thomason and Corrie, Brown and Marshman, the Sherwoods and the Youngs – all these who had loved him and shared his devotion to Christ belonged to the past, and his lot now lay with British officials and politicians, whose help he needed and whose respect he gained.

Yet it was never in European society that Henry was most at ease. At night in Bombay he was to be found walking on the beach with Ezra, an imposing Persian Jew longing for the restoration to Jerusalem, or locked in discussion with Mahomet Jan, a youth speaking beautiful Persian whose mind seemed open to persuasion. 'I am visited from morning till night by the learned natives, who are drawn here by an Arabic tract which I composed to help Sabat but which the scribe I employed has been showing all round.'

His most exacting encounter was with Feeroz, 'who is considered the most learned man here. He spoke Persian, was familiar with Arabic, and began by saying that no one religion had more evidence for its truth than another, for all the miracles of their respective founders depended on tradition – which I denied.' As a Persian he pressed Henry to tell him from what country the wise men who saw the star had come. 'I asked him whether he had any thought of changing his religion. With a contemptuous smile he said, "No, every man is safe in his own religion",

so I asked him what sinners must do to obtain pardon.'
While Feeroz claimed that repentance was enough,
Henry argued that the atonement of Christ was essential,
to which Feeroz answered that Muslims believed Husain
was an atonement for the sins of men. He found fault
with the Persian New Testament on Henry's table, asking
why it was not made in the current form of the language.

Next day Feeroz was back to read to Henry a poem he
had written on the conquest of India by the British.
Henry was impressed with his patience, 'one of the most
agreeable qualities a disputant can possess. He never
interrupted me and if I rudely interrupted him he was
silent in a moment.' It was the first of many stiff dia-
logues with Persian intellectuals. The old man argued
with him about the eternity of God and of matter, the
authorship of the Pentateuch, and the truth of the Genesis account of the origin of things. 'Jews and Christians
charge Muslims with cruelty in propagating religion by
the sword,' he said, 'but was not Moses a warrior? Christ
was meek and lowly, a poor man till his death, but did
not the Portuguese use force in India to convert the
Hindus? Anyway, Christians all disagree with one another and the Portuguese say the English will perish.'
When Henry tried to explain about the Reformation,
Feeroz cut him short, 'Yes, I know, that was in the reign
of Henry VIII.' They could not agree about the devil:
'I believe in no such person,' said Feeroz. 'God is all-
powerful, so why does he not destroy him?' All the New
Testament versions Henry showed him he condemned.
Opening a chapter in Sabat's Persian translation he
pointed out various errors and laughed at some of the
Arabic words. Henry told him the translator was an
Arab who had lived for ten years in Persia. 'An Arab,'
rejoined Feeroz, 'if he live there twenty years, will never
speak Persian well.'

This friendship then had to terminate. It was six

months since Henry had left the settled life of Cawnpore and he kept writing nostalgically to Corrie. 'To move from place to place, hurried away without having time to do good, is vexatious to the spirit and harassing to the body. The sea, too, I loathe.' But on 25 March 1811, he embarked in a vessel whose mission was described as 'Operations against Arab pirates in the Persian Gulf'.

16 Uphill all the way to Shiraz

The crossing from Bombay to Muscat in Arabia took
twenty-seven days. As usual Henry was sea-sick, but then
the weather relented and this last of his ocean voyages
became the pleasantest. There were over fifty Europeans
on board: gunners and sailors, mostly Spanish, French
and Portuguese. As the pirates kept out of their way the
voyage was uneventful. Every night Henry conducted
Bible reading and prayers in the main cabin. Daily he
was thrown together with Captain Sealy and his cousin,
Captain Lockett, who was in command of the gunners.
'They are a kind of men I have not often met with. They
don't seem to feel at all in religion, never speak about it,
and show no interest in what I say to them. Yet they read
their Bibles each morning, pray at nights, and avoid
everything immoral in their conversation.'

They were a week at Muscat. 'In a small cove, surrounded by bare rocks heated through and through, out
of the reach of air as well as wind, lies the good ship
Benares, in the great cabin of which, stretched out on a
couch, lie I, weak but well.' In fact he had plenty of time
at his disposal on this trip and wasted too much of it in
speculations about the Hebrew language which always
left him unsatisfied. 'All the way, as usual, I have been
Hebraizing. I resolve to read Arabic or Persian but before I am aware of it I am thinking about Hebrew. I have
translated Psalm 16 and, except that one part lacks support, I should have sent it to that obstinate lover of

antiquity, Thomas Thomason, whose potent touch has dissolved so many of my fabrics that I don't like to submit anything to him which is not foolproof.'

Henry suffered from the lack of such a friend at close quarters and Hebrew remained the one area in which his linguistic gift was somewhat undisciplined. His real genius was for New Testament translation and he needed advice to stick to what he could do best. 'The further I push my enquiries the more I am distressed. My prayer must be, "Lord, teach me just as much as thou seest is good for me." I thank God for Sir Isaac Newton who, beginning with the things next to him, and humbly and quietly moving to the things next to them, enlarged the boundaries of human knowledge more than the rest of the sons of men. God has thus given us the example of one who sought knowledge temperately and whom he blessed with success.'

The area around Muscat was unsafe, so movement on shore was discouraged. Henry and Captain Lockett walked through the bazaar and an Arab soldier accompanied them to see a garden a mile away, which was regarded as a great marvel in such a wilderness. The Arab had an African slave who attached himself to Henry and argued vigorously for Islam. Next day the Arab and the African came to see him on board. 'The instant I gave them a Gospel in Arabic the African began to read it and carried it off as a great prize.' But in spite of his dreams and hopes, that was all Henry was ever able to do for Christ in Arabia.

The next three weeks were spent crossing over to the Persian coast and struggling slowly up the Gulf, tossed by a strong gale. He did his best to write to Lydia. 'When will our correspondence be established? I have been trying to effect it these six years. But I am not yet without hope that a letter in the beloved hand will overtake me

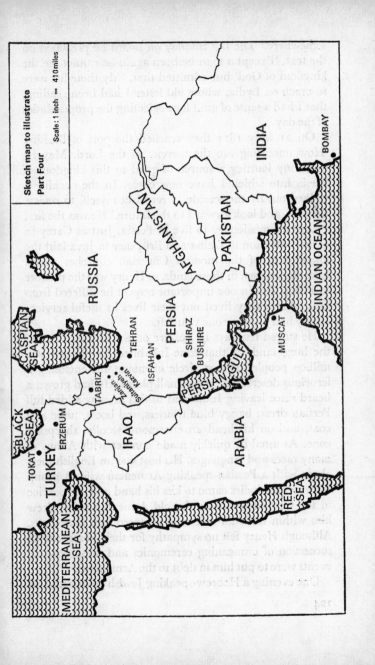

Sketch map to illustrate
Part Four

Scale: 1 inch = 410 miles

somewhere.' The last Sunday on board he preached on the text, 'Except a man be born again he cannot see the kingdom of God' but admitted that, 'My thoughts were so much on Lydia, whose old letter I had been reading, that I had a sense of guilt for neglecting the proper duties of the day.'

On 21 May 1811 they reached the port of Bushire. 'How unceasing are the mercies of the Lord. May he make my journey a source of good to this kingdom of Persia into which I have now come. In the evening I walked out by the seaside to recollect myself, to review the past, and look forward to the future.' He was the first Protestant missionary to live in Persia. Just as Carey in India, Morrison in China and Brückner in Java laid the foundations of the modern Christian churches which have since arisen in those lands, so Henry was the pioneer in Persia. But in one important respect he differed from those three: they lived out their lives in useful service; Henry had just over one year left.

He stayed ten days in Bushire on the southern rim of the huge land, at that time inhabited by about seven million people, its vast circle of mountains enclosing a ferocious desert fringed by small plains. He had grown a beard since leaving India and to this he now added full Persian dress: baggy blue trousers, red boots, tunic and coat, and on his head an enormous, woolly, sheepskin cone. As usual he quickly made contact with Asians of many races and languages. His host was an English merchant with a Persian-speaking Armenian wife. A group of Armenian ladies came to kiss his hand and at a service in the Orthodox church the old Armenian priest drew him within the altar rails and incensed him four times. Although Henry felt no sympathy for their 'disagreeable succession of unmeaning ceremonies and noisy chants', events were to put him in debt to the Armenians.

One evening a Hebrew-speaking Jewish goldsmith and

his son called on him. 'Grief has marked the countenance of the eastern Jews in a way that makes them indescribably interesting. I could have wept while looking at them. They are as much oppressed in Persia as ever. Their women are not allowed to veil, as all others are required to do, so if one is more than ordinarily beautiful she is soon sent for, made a Muslim, and put into a harem.'

When Henry showed four different Arabic versions of Matthew's Gospel to a learned Arab he at once picked out Sabat's, saying, 'This is good, very good.' As the news spread that an unusual European linguist had appeared, a prominent Turk also came to test Henry's Arabic. The Persian Governor treated him with marked respect: they discussed both the art of colouring glass and the legitimacy of Muslims having paintings of the Virgin and Child.

But no close friendships were made in those few days, so that Henry was more alone than he had ever been in his life when on the evening of 30 May 1811 he rode out of the gate of Bushire in a caravan of thirty horses and mules bound for Shiraz, 170 miles away in the Zagros Mountains. 'It was a fine moonlight night, the scene new and perfectly oriental. I felt a little melancholy but commended myself to God and was assured of his presence. As the night advanced one of the muleteers began to sing in a voice so plaintive that everyone's attention was arrested. When he paused nothing was heard but the tinkling of the bells on the necks of the mules. His first line was enough for me – "Think not that e'er my heart can dwell contented far from thee." It is what I have often felt when setting out on a journey.' He rode a pony, his belongings were on a mule, and he was accompanied by his Armenian servant, Zechariah, whose talkativeness made him a general source of amusement.

In spite of this romantic start the rest of the ten-day journey to Shiraz was a terrible ordeal for Henry. They travelled only by night, lying up by day as best they could to shelter from the fearful heat. He soon realized he might not survive such conditions. Lack of sleep, fear of scorpions, and burning fever tormented him. He spent the days with his head wrapped in a wet towel. On the fourth night they ascended the first big ledge of mountains. In his stupefied state Henry let the reins fall loose on his pony's neck, trusting the animal to find its way safely beside tremendous precipices. The next night they mounted another huge ridge on to a high plateau where they shivered in the cold. When they reached the town of Kazarun 'there seemed to be a fire in my head, my skin was like cinder, and my pulse violent. Through the day it was again too hot to sleep, though the place we occupied was a summer house in a garden of cypress trees. Had the caravan gone on the next night I could not have accompanied it, but it did not, so I got a sort of night's rest, though I woke twenty times to dip my burning hands in water.'

On beyond, in the high valleys of the Zagros Mountains, Henry revived a little among fields of wheat and barley, where large herds of cattle browsed and the temperature was like spring in England. 'A few hours sleep restored me from the stupidity in which I had been for several days. I awoke with a light heart and said, "He knoweth our frame and remembereth we are dust. He redeemeth our life from destruction. He maketh us to lie down in green pastures. And when we have left this vale of tears there shall be no more sorrow nor any more pain, the sun shall not light upon thee nor any heat, but the Lamb shall lead thee to living fountains of waters." '

By the morning of 9 June, they were outside the walls of Shiraz. Nearby was the camp of Sir Gore Ouseley, the British Ambassador. 'In the evening we dined with his Excellency, who gave us a general invitation to his table.'

For eleven months Henry stayed in Shiraz, the famous city of medieval poets, set in barren mountains. Though perpetually surrounded by crowds of people and engaged in intensive translation work and long arguments with Sufis, the mystics of Islam, he was none the less isolated, lacking a single friend who shared his outlook. The Christians he found were mostly Christians in the racial and cultural sense: Armenians and Russians from the Orthodox tradition, minority groups in Persia, for whom aggressive dialogue with Muslims would have been dangerous. He alone was free to say what he liked, and soon Zechariah assured him he was the talk of the town. 'It is rumoured I have come to Shiraz to become a Muslim and then to bring in five thousand men from India on pretence of making them Muslims too, but in reality to take the city.'

Yet the fact that he was European was also a protection to him. Sir John Malcolm's introduction gave him favour with Sir Gore Ouseley, who remained for some weeks in Shiraz. Henry preached to Sir Gore's household and baptized his child. Together they called upon Prince Abbas Mirza, son of the Shah of Persia. Sir Gore's secretary was a Mr Morier, so Henry suggested to Lydia that she should send a letter ahead of him, addressed care of Morier's father in Constantinople, which thus loomed on the horizon of his life for the first time.

Thanks again to Sir John Malcolm he was also welcomed by a prominent citizen of Shiraz, Jaffir Ali, in whose house he lived. Jaffir Ali introduced him to his brother-in-law, Seid Ali, with whom he worked every day translating the New Testament and Psalms into Persian. Both these men were rather open-minded Sufis who treated Henry with remarkable kindness. In his friendless position this was invaluable. Just as a change from city life, Jaffir Ali pitched a tent for him by a stream outside the walls. When boys continually threw stones at him on his daily ride, Jaffir Ali reported it to the Governor of the city, who called on Henry in person and gave orders that in future anyone who insulted him was to be bastinadoed. And out of respect for Sir John Malcolm one of Persia's most renowned Generals came to see him.

All this could expose Henry to the charge that he aligned himself with western imperialism and its political agents. Yet his one desire was to serve Christ and spread the gospel. He was not in the least concerned to promote British interests and his message was normally very unpopular with his own countrymen. But he lived in a pioneer age when there were no missionary societies in Persia to help him. He had no contacts of his own and no previous knowledge of the country. A world war was raging. Travel was incredibly difficult. He was in poor health and far beyond the reach of skilled medical aid. The gulf in living standards and in mentality between East and West was also greater then than now. So he was thankful for any assistance he could get which would enable him to exist in Persia and carry out his task of Bible translation.

He spared a day to visit nearby Persepolis, riding both ways by night. Unaccustomed to tourists, and seeing his eyes, red with cold and lack of sleep, people thought he was escaping to an uninhabited spot in order to drink freely. Weary though he was, he remained alert enough to seize any opportunity to reveal his faith to his travelling companions. They relied on him to show them the direction of Mecca for their morning prayers. Suddenly one of them said to him, 'Sir, what is the chief good of life?'

'The love of God,' said Henry.

'What next?'

'The love of man.'

'To have men love us, or to love them?'

'To love them,' he replied.

128

Barely had he settled into Shiraz when Henry realized that he would have to scrap the Persian New Testament on which he and Sabat had worked in Cawnpore and produce an entirely new one with the aid of Seid Ali. This time there were no British regiments to minister to, so he gave himself utterly to that one task, diverted only by heated discussions with the Muslim intelligentsia. His plans had been so uncertain since he left Calcutta that mail had long ceased to reach him, so the arrival of letters from Corrie was a great delight. In reply he poured out the story of his struggles. 'I am trying to learn the true use of time by placing myself twenty years in advance and then considering how I ought to have managed twenty years ago. In racing violently for a year or two and then breaking down? In this way I have reasoned myself into contentment about staying in Shiraz. I thought at first, what will the Government of India think of my being away so long? What will my friends think? Shall I not appear to all a wandering shepherd, leaving the flock and running about for my own pleasure? But, placing myself twenty years on in time, I say, why could I not have remained long enough in Shiraz to get a New Testament done? What work of equal importance can ever come from me? So now I am resolved to wait here till the New Testament is finished. I go on as usual, riding round the walls in the morning and singing hymns at night over my milk and water – for tea I have none, though I want it. I am with you in spirit almost every evening and feel one with the saints of God all over the earth.'

17 Controversy and triumph

There was quite a colony of Jews in Shiraz. One of them, who had become a Muslim, informed Henry that he had found a reference to Muhammad in the book of Deuteronomy, quoting the verse, 'I will raise them up a Prophet from among their brethren.' This man, who had taken the name of Abdul Ghunee, had a heated public discussion with Henry declaring he could find nothing in the Gospels about the atonement. He came back again and again. 'Abdul Ghunee stayed the whole morning and asked many questions. He showed himself extremely well-read in the Hebrew Bible and the Koran, quoting both with the utmost readiness. He said he must come every day and either make me a Muslim or become a Christian himself. I told him, God has indeed raised up a great Prophet from the midst of you, Jesus, but you have gone after a stranger from a nation who were always your enemies.'

Months later, as Henry walked in a garden, Abdul Ghunee asked him what would become of Muslim Jews in the next world. He suggested Muslims might be right in their way, and Christians in theirs, but what could such as he expect? He asked if Henry thought it would be safe to throw off the Muslim mask in Baghdad. 'Feelings of pity for God's ancient people, and the seriousness of his enquiry, relieved me from the pressure of my own comparatively insignificant distresses. I, a poor Gentile, am blessed, loved, and secured by the everlasting covenant, while the children of the kingdom are still lying in outer darkness.'

Noticing a dozen Jews with their rabbi one day, he could not resist the temptation. 'I attacked them and disputed a little on Psalms 2, 16 and 24. They were utterly unacquainted with Jesus and surprised at what I told them about his resurrection and ascension. The rabbi abruptly broke off the conversation, told me he would talk with me in my room, and carried away his flock.'

Much less cordial disputes with others were a daily occurrence. Youths schooled in Sufism came to try him with hard questions about the nature of being. The Prince's secretary argued that every created thing, including Henry himself, was itself God. A man who had abandoned Islam advised Henry to throw off his Christian yoke too. 'I told him I preferred my yoke to his freedom. He was for sending me naked into a wilderness, but I would rather be a child under the restraints of a parent who would be my protector and guide. To everything I said he had but one answer, that God is the sole agent, so that sin and holiness, happiness and misery, cause and effect, heaven and hell, are all perfectly one.'

Later on a public debate was arranged between Henry and a Professor of Muslim Law. They sat on a high platform covered with carpets beside a pond in a fine courtyard. Surrounded by his learned friends, the Professor gave an opening speech which lasted several hours. 'After clearing his way for miles around, he announced that philosophers had proved that a single Being could produce but a single being.' By the time he was silent many of the audience had gone, Henry was sleepy, and there had been no meeting of minds.

A prominent Muslim teacher, Ibrahim, to whose

uprightness and kindness to the poor Henry bore witness, then published an elaborate defence of Islam. In his written reply Henry did not hesitate to say that Muhammad did no miracles, spread his religion by purely human means, framed his precepts and promises to gratify men's sensuality, and was ambitious for himself and his family. He declared that the Koran was full of absurdities and contradictions, encouraged a spirit of cruelty and extermination, and advocated a way of salvation which was wholly ineffective in contrast to the glorious gospel and atonement of Jesus Christ.

Chancing one day to find Ibrahim lecturing in the centre of a large company of scholars, Henry asked permission to speak. This was given, in the hope that he might be converted to Islam, so he was called up to an empty seat close to the lecturer. 'After the usual compliments he asked me without further ceremony what we meant by calling Christ God. War being thus declared, I had nothing to do but to stand on the defensive. Ibrahim argued temperately enough but some of the others were very violent. He asked me if Christ was the Creator or a creature. I replied, "The Creator".'

Afterwards Ibrahim came to see him privately and asked, 'How could sins be atoned for before they were committed? If Jesus died for all, will all necessarily be saved? And if faith is the condition of salvation, will wicked Christians be saved provided they believe?' 'To this last objection I remarked that to those who felt themselves sinners and came to God for mercy through Christ, God would give his Holy Spirit, which would progressively sanctify them in heart and life.'

When Prince Abbas Mirza himself enquired what were the laws of Christianity, Henry quoted, 'Thou shalt love the Lord thy God with all thy heart, and thy neighbour as thyself.' The Prince's reaction was, 'What could be better?' but his nephew, angered by Henry's attack on Muhammad, observed that the proper answer to it was the sword.

The Prime Minister of the province of Fars, in which Shiraz lay, came in the presence of a large crowd to question Henry about European philosophy, but was soon out of his depth in astronomy and mathematics. One after another the scholars of Shiraz tilted at him, often trying to prove that 'since all being is an emanation of the Deity, the will of every being is only the will of the Deity'.

An old philosopher with a silvery beard invited him to his house one evening. After sitting for a long time in total silence Henry was told, 'It is the custom here to think much and speak little.' In the end he took the initiative and asked, 'What is the way to be happy?' The sage replied that the shortest way to happiness was the subjugation of the passions. Six weeks later the old man returned Henry's call. 'I plied him with innumerable questions but only got incoherent answers. Then, laying aside his turban, he put on his night-cap and soon fell asleep on the carpet. While he lay there his disciples came. When I told them they would not believe it till they came in and saw him. The real state of this man seems to be despair. I preached to him the kingdom of God, mentioning how I had found peace myself, forgiveness through the Son of God, and sanctification through the Spirit of God.'

Though Henry acknowledged that 'frigid reasoning with men of perverse minds seldom brings people to Christ' and that the best arguments are powerless until the Holy Spirit makes them effective, he was not altogether discouraged. 'Persia is a field ripe for harvest. Vast numbers secretly despise the superstition imposed on them. As many as have heard the gospel approve it but dare not hazard their lives for the name of the Lord Jesus. Sometimes I have been asked if the external appearance of Islam could not be retained along with Christianity, and whether I could not baptize them without them having to believe in the deity of Christ. I tell them, No.' He regarded the translation of the New Testament as paving the way for future Persian Christians: 'Perhaps we witness the dawn of the day of glory.'

Now and again he wrote wistfully to Lydia. 'It is true that I cannot look back upon many days, nor even many hours, passed with you. But we have insensibly become more acquainted with each other so that, on my part at least, separation has brought us nearer. To know that there is one who is willing to think of me is soothing to a degree none can know but those who have lost all their relations. I am in perfect health, but I fancy my spirits would be better were the beloved Persis by my side. This name, which I once gave you, occurs to me at this moment I suppose because I am in Persia, entrenched in one of its valleys, separated from friends in India by chains of mountains and a roaring sea, among a people depraved beyond belief, in the power of a tyrant guilty of every atrocity. Imagine a pale person with a formidable moustache, dressed as a Persian, seated on a Persian carpet in a room without table or chair, and you see me. My host, Jaffir Ali, tries to make the period of my captivity as agreeable as possible. His wife never appears. I must say that society here, from the exclusion of women, is as dull as it can well be. Yet I have reason to rejoice at being sent here. There is such an extraordinary stir about religion throughout the city, that some good must come of it. Yet I sometimes sigh for a little Christian fellowship. I have seen European newspapers only four months old, so I am delightfully near you. Pray that utterance may be given me, that I may open my mouth boldly to make known the mystery of the gospel. Remember me with the most unfeigned affection to all my dear friends. This is now the seventh letter I have sent you without having received an answer.'

In his ninth unanswered letter he admitted, 'I think of you incessantly, too much I fear. In prayer I often feel what you described five years ago, a particular pleasure in regarding you as with me before the Lord. When I sit and muse my spirit flies away and joins you in Marazion. If you acknowledge a kindred feeling still, we are not separated; our spirits have met and blended.'

Now that he was far from India, 'the country I have come to regard as my own', he was inclined to compare it favourably with 'this miserable country', and relieved his feelings by long letters to Corrie. 'I am often tempted to get away from this prison. I can conceive of no greater happiness than to be settled for life in India, superintending schools as we did.' More than once he tried to escape. It was planned that Seid Ali and his family should accompany him to Baghdad, but the route proved unsafe. Then, lacking a friend with whom to consult, Henry conceived the notion of going north into Armenia, through the Caucasus Mountains to Turkey, and then back south into Syria. But it appeared the Persian army was moving against the Turks, so he remained anchored in Shiraz at his task of translation.

At Christmas, 1811, he gave a feast for the Armenians. Shortly afterwards one of them was arrested by the Persian authorities and the Armenian community appealed to Henry for help. He himself could not do much, but Jaffir Ali succeeded in getting the man released. The Armenians attributed this to Henry. 'They were in ecstasies of joy and did not know how to express their gratitude. These unfortunate people have been treated almost like the Jews. If an Armenian gets a new coat he patches the sleeves, as it is sure to be taken from him if it looks new.' As a result of this incident two Armenians came to discuss with Henry how to reconcile the biblical promises of salvation by faith with such texts as, 'Every idle word that men shall speak they shall give account thereof in the day of judgment.'

As was his custom, Henry reviewed his life at the end of 1811. 'It has been a memorable year. I like to be usefully employed in a way I did not expect, specially if my own will is to some extent crossed by the work, as then there is reason to believe that God is acting. Whether I live to finish the Persian New Testament or not, my life is of little consequence. I look back with shame upon the time when I attached importance to my own life and labours. Clumsiness mars all the works of man. I am relieved only by thinking that we have a city whose builder and maker is God. The least of his works is refreshing to look at, even a dried leaf or a straw. But whether life or death be mine, may Christ be magnified in me. If he has work for me to do I cannot die.'

Month after month Seid Ali sat with Henry translating the New Testament, just as Sabat had done in India. Whereas Sabat had been a professing Christian, Seid Ali was a Muslim, but he was very much easier for Henry to work with. From childhood he had been looking for a sure religion. The Europeans he had previously met had been soldiers with no interest in such matters. Henry was the first man of another faith with whom he had had the chance to talk frankly. 'You must not regret the loss of the time you give me,' he said, 'because it does me good.'

The idea of the new birth appealed to him. He longed to be certain that he would be given the Holy Spirit. 'How Christ loved those twelve people,' he remarked.

'Yes', answered Henry, 'and all those who believe in him too.' But Seid Ali was hedged in by the traditions in which he had been reared, the idea that there is no real difference between good and evil, and that all things are only so many forms of God. He was tormented by the tension between these philosophical principles and the teaching of the New Testament. 'In these doubts he is tossed to and fro and often kept awake the whole night in tears. He and his brother talk on these things till they are almost crazed.'

'Would you have me believe like a child?' he asked Henry. 'Truly I think that would be the only way.' He was amazed that Christians could speak so confidently of being saved. 'The truth is', he suggested, 'we are in a state of compound ignorance, ignorant, yet ignorant of our ignorance.' But as his knowledge of the New Testament increased he pressed Henry hard, agreeing with the scoffers in the Second Epistle of Peter. 'They are right! Where are any of his promises fulfilled? Christian nations are nothing compared to Arabia, Persia, India and Turkey. And professing Christians who deny the deity of Christ and treat the atonement as a fable are also right. It is contrary to reason that one person should be an atonement for all the rest, and it is nowhere stated in the Gospels. Christ said he was sent only to the lost sheep of the house of Israel. Can you give me a proof of Christianity that I may believe or be left without excuse if I don't, a proof like one of the theorems of Euclid?' But whatever his doubts he stuck to the job with Henry till the work was done.

On 12 February 1812, the Persian New Testament was finished. Three weeks later the Book of Psalms was also completed. 'Seid Ali never argues against the truth now,' said Henry. 'He speaks of his dislike of the drunken habits of some of the Sufis, and this approach to the love of morality is the best sign of a change I have seen in him yet. He always produces the New Testament when any of his friends come. They ridicule him, but he tells them it is certainly better to have gained all this information about the religion of the Christians than to have loitered away the year in the gardens.'

Henry remained in Shiraz until 11 May, chiefly to supervise the task of making several copies of the New Testament manuscript. Shortly before he left he was visited by a young man named Muhammad Rahim who had previously often come with others to oppose and ridicule the gospel. However, every interview had tended to increase his respect for Henry and to diminish his confidence in Islam. He was amazed not only at Henry's excellent Persian, but also at his patience and the calm, convincing way in which he argued. Gradually he came to feel that Henry was right, but then he was afraid of what others would say, so he avoided him for some months. At the end 'I could not refrain from paying him a farewell visit. Our conversation, the memory of which will never fade from my mind, sealed my conversion. He gave me a book which has been my constant companion. The study of it has formed my most delightful occupation.' Long afterwards he showed it to a Christian visitor. On the flyleaf was written, 'There is joy in heaven over one sinner that repenteth. Henry Martyn.'

As the time for parting drew near, Seid Ali's affection for Henry seemed to increase. He and Jaffir Ali asked him to read them some of the Old Testament history and this took up several days. He admitted that he had been impressed by the contrast between the early spread of the gospel as recorded in the Acts of the Apostles and the beginnings of the expansion of Islam, when men were murdered and caravans were robbed. On their last day together Henry explained to him what to do with the precious manuscripts of the New Testament in case he himself died, and exhorted him 'as far as his confessions allowed me, to stand fast'.

18 The last friend

Henry finally left Shiraz for Tehran in a company which
included the Rev. William Canning, the new chaplain
for the British Embassy. He planned to present a manuscript copy of the New Testament to the Shah. He took
two with him, leaving several others with Seid Ali. This
decision to go north was the most fateful he ever made.
At no time in his life did he so much need a companion
with whom to talk over his affairs. For until the New
Testament was printed it could be read by very few
people. Only a few years later his counterpart in Java,
Gottlob Brückner, having translated it into Javanese took
ship for India to have it printed by the Baptist missionaries at Serampore. He then returned in triumph to Java
with three thousand copies.

It would have been wise of Henry to have done the
same. He had often longed to be back in India, whereas
to present a copy to the Shah was a dramatic act of
limited value. He was in much better health, having been
spared intense heat at five thousand feet above sea level
in Shiraz. And in that whole year he had preached only
one sermon, the day he addressed the British Ambassador's household. Even the long arguments with Muslims
had not tried his lungs as much as the four Sunday sermons in Cawnpore, and there is scarcely a reference to
pain in the chest during his Shiraz days. He was no
longer obviously facing an early death. His unique
linguistic gifts might have flowered still more if he could

have returned to Calcutta, seen the Persian New Testament through the press, and then gone home to marry Lydia before giving his mind to new duties in Asia. It was only 170 miles back to Bushire and the chance of a ship to Bombay.

Instead he rode north. Then one circumstance after another drew him on towards the Caucasus Mountains. The only logical exit from such a route was Constantinople, three thousand miles ahead. But, as Fitzgerald's version of Omar Khayyám's stanza so incomparably expressed it,

> 'The Moving Finger writes; and, having writ,
> Moves on: nor all thy Piety nor Wit
> Shall lure it back to cancel half a Line,
> Nor all thy Tears wash out a Word of it.'

Passing by Persepolis and the tomb of Cyprus the Great, they crossed a vast plain, empty but for the black tents of nomads, dwarfed by jagged ranges of treeless mountains. On the eleventh day they reached Isfahan and lodged in one of the Shah's palaces.

Next day Henry crossed the river to call on the Armenian bishops at Jolfa, the greatest concentration of Armenians in Persia. But he was not one to sympathize much with 'pageantry, processions, ringing of bells, waving of colours, and other ceremonies so numerous as to remove all semblance of true worship'. A week later they moved on, and came after ten days to Tehran. It was a relatively easy trip and Henry found time both to correct his manuscripts and to enjoy a nightingale's song as they passed through deep woods by the light of the moon. At some village caravanserai on the edge of the desert a crowd gathered round him, 'asking questions about Europe and interrogating me concerning Christ till I mounted my horse and rode from among them'. Some hours before dawn they came to the walls of Tehran. 'I spread my bed upon the high road and slept till the gates were opened, then entered the city and took up my abode at the ambassador's residence.'

However, Sir Gore was not there. He was far on to the north-west at Tabriz. Nor was the Shah in Tehran. His camp was at Karaz, one stage towards Tabriz. Since Jaffir Ali had given Henry a letter of introduction to the Prime Minister, he decided to go to Karaz, travelling through another night. On arrival in the morning he found the Prime Minister lying ill on the verandah of the Shah's tent of audience. And that verandah was the nearest Henry ever got to the Shah.

The Prime Minister and two of the royal secretaries had a long conversation with him about religion and metaphysics. They plied him with questions. 'What are the principles of your religion? What is the state of the soul after death? Have you read the Koran? What do you say to the divisions of the moon? What are your notions on this extraordinary subject, the Trinity?'

Manuscript in hand, Henry stayed day after day in Karaz in hopes of seeing the Shah. Instead he came to the most dangerous moment in his life since the drunken soldier had threatened him in South Africa. In the presence of the Prime Minister he became the centre of a group of bitterly hostile scholars. 'You had better say God is God and Muhammad is the Prophet of God,' they said. But he answered, 'God is God and Jesus is the Son of God.' In a tumult of anger and disgust they rose up shouting, 'He is neither born nor begets', and seemed about to tear him in pieces. One of them yelled, 'What will you say when your tongue is burnt out for this blasphemy?' but not all agreed with the severity of this remark. 'My book, which I had expected to present to the Shah, lay there before the Prime Minister. I was afraid they would trample on it, so I went in among them, picked it up, and wrapped it in a towel before them, while they looked at me with supreme contempt. I walked away alone to pass the rest of the day in heat and dirt. What have I done, thought I, to merit all this scorn? Nothing but bear testimony to Jesus. I thought over these things in prayer and my troubled heart found that peace which Christ promised to his disciples. But a message came to say it was not the Shah's custom to receive any Englishman unless presented by the ambassador; I must therefore wait till the Shah reached Sultaniyeh, where the Ambassador would be.'

Sultaniyeh was another 150 miles north-west towards Tabriz. Rejoined by William Canning, Henry started off at once. They reached Kazvin and he sat down in the dust on the shady side of a walled village 'and sighed at the thought of my dear friends in India and England. What vast regions I must traverse before I can get to either! I comfort myself with the hope that God has something for me to do by thus delaying my exit.' At last he seemed to realize how far off course he was, how totally land-locked, how remote from any possibility of exit at all.

In Kazvin they were not at all welcome, for everyone was shortly expecting the Shah. It was cold there, even at midday: an icy wind was blowing over the mountains from the Caspian Sea. 'I thought of nothing but my friends in England and the days when I walked with them in weather like this. I had them all in my mind and bore them upon my heart in prayer.'

Sultaniyeh was no better. At the caravanserai the Shah's servants had already taken possession of the guest room and seemed to enjoy the chance to humble Europeans. 'All along the road the people are patiently waiting as for some dreadful disaster, the misery of being subjected to the violence of rabble soldiery.' There was no sign of the ambassador, so all they could do was to go on to Tabriz.

At Zanjan, 150 miles from their goal, Henry 'rose so ill with fever that I could not go on'. The next twelve days were one long nightmare. Canning was ill too and their money running out. With remarkable kindness a humble muleteer became security for them. But Henry grew worse, 'tortured with shocking pains in the head till I was almost frantic.' Through thunderstorms and hail they managed to move slowly ahead and he contrived to keep up his journal. 'We are approaching the boundaries of Parthia and Media, and a most natural boundary it is, as the two ridges of mountain we have had on the left and right come round and form a barrier.' Into this barrier they moved in the night, with Henry past all clear thought. For a while they lost him as he lay down next day under the shade of a bridge with some camel drivers. 'Want of sleep, want of food and exposure to the sun put me in a high fever which raged furiously all day. I almost despaired of getting alive through this unfortunate journey.' In the pre-dawn twilight of 6 July he struggled on alone in hopes of getting to the city before the terrible sun rose again. 'Some of the people seemed to feel compassion for me and asked if I was not very ill. At last I reached the gate and asked a man to show me the way to the ambassador's house.' It was fifty-seven days since he had left Shiraz.

Life was repeating itself. He had staggered into Cawnpore like that and been saved by the Sherwoods. Now, in even worse condition, he was rescued by another friendly home. A Government official overseas is not necessarily pleased when a missionary at the point of death collapses on his doorstep. We do not know what Sir Gore and Lady Ouseley really thought about it all, but there is no doubt that they rose to the occasion with outstanding kindness. The royal family had commandeered the house of Tabriz's richest citizen as a temporary residence for the British Ambassador, who was then engaged in delicate mediation between Persia and Turkey. For two months Henry stayed there, very weak and ill.

'For a long time every species of medicine was tried in vain. Incessant headaches allowed me no rest, day or night.' Although we know that a doctor attended him, his journal does not record a single incident of his stay, nor anything about Sir Gore and Lady Ouseley beyond the mere fact that they took him in. He soon realized that it was impossible to retrace his steps to India and that he must apply for furlough in England. On 12 July he wrote to inform Lydia and to acknowledge a letter which he had just received from her, the first for eighteen months. 'Why have you not written more about yourself?' he asked her, and then added, 'I must faithfully tell you that the probability of my reaching England alive is but small.' The same day he wrote at greater length to Simeon, fearing that he might not approve of his return – 'but you would, were you to see the pitiable condition to which I am reduced and knew what it is to traverse the continent of Asia in the destitute state in which I am. I think it most probable that you will not see me, the way ahead being not better than that passed over, which has nearly killed me. I would not pain your heart, my dear brother, but we who are in Jesus have the privilege of viewing life and death as nearly the same, since both are one. Nothing seemingly remains for me to do but to follow the rest of my family to the tomb.'

On 20 August his fever abated and he recovered his strength. Instead of giving himself the chance to convalesce, 'I immediately began to gird up my loins and prepare for my journey.' Within only thirteen days he had left the shelter of Tabriz. Sir Gore advised him to go through Armenia and Turkey to Constantinople, as he could give introductions to important people over at least the first half of this route. He also secured good horses for Henry, and a guard.

He wrote a final letter to Lydia on 28 August, warning her again that he might not survive. 'I am still at a tremendous distance and many of the countries I have to pass through are dangerous to the traveller. Ignorant as I am of Turkish, my case would be pitiable indeed if I should be taken ill on the road, but I trust I shall shortly see thee face to face.'

It was 1,500 miles from Tabriz to Constantinople. And this time there was no friendly home on the route at all.

19 Overdue at Constantinople

At sunset on 2 September 1812, Henry rode out of Tabriz with Sergius his Armenian servant, a Persian guard, and two horses carrying his baggage. 'I looked around the creation with delight. It is necessary to have been confined to bed to know the joy of moving freely through the works of God.'

Conditions were rough and he was often lodged in stables where mosquitoes, vermin and stench contested sleep. To avoid the heat they usually travelled from midnight to sunrise, while Henry filled his mind with the fourteenth, fifteenth and sixteenth Psalms in Hebrew. Before dawn on the fifth day they reached the Araxes River, today the border between Russia and Persia – though at that time both banks were Persian. At first light they crossed by ferry and as they rode on till noon in the hot sun Henry's attention became riveted to a towering, snow-capped mountain ahead. It was Ararat. 'On the peak of that hill the whole church was once contained; now it has spread far and wide to the ends of the earth.' But they lost their way, the baggage horses stumbled into water, and some of his books got spoilt. Two bearded old men kindly opened their home to the little party and made a fire at dead of night to dry the books.

East of the Araxes they came to Erevan, now the capital of the Armenian Soviet Socialist Republic, but then still in Persia. Henry had an introduction from Sir

Gore to the Governor, a powerful person surrounded by richly dressed servants, who went on reading the Koran and took not the slightest notice of Henry or the ambassador's letter. When it was eventually read to him he became attentive and granted Henry a private interview.

Next day, 12 September, Henry rode ahead alone to Etschmiadzin, the religious capital of the Armenians since AD 300. He made for a very large church surrounded by a wall, where he found monks in the courtyard. Again he produced Sir Gore's letters, written this time in Armenian and addressed to the Patriarch and to Bishop Nestus. He was at once escorted to the Patriarch's house where he found two bishops at breakfast, Nestus and Serope, a man of his own age, fluent in French, Italian and English. With the Patriarch mostly in bed, and Nestus rigid in his thinking, Henry soon found that Serope was his man.

Born an Armenian Catholic and educated at Rome, Serope had been disillusioned with Catholicism during a visit to Lebanon. After being recalled to Etschmiadzin to train men for the ministry, it became his ambition to reform the archaic Armenian Orthodox Church: to purge it of superstition and traditionalism by teaching logic and science in the seminary. Henry said all he could to encourage him, 'proving to him from the example of Luther and the European reformers that God would be with him however arduous the work might be'.

An audience with the Patriarch followed. 'He was reclining on a sort of throne in the middle of the room. A chair was set close to him for me and Serope stood by to interpret. The Patriarch expressed his hopes of deliverance from the Muslim yoke. He asked about my Scripture translation and told me to consider myself at home in the monastery. Indeed their attention and kindness are unbounded. Nestus and Serope anticipate my every wish. I told the Patriarch I was so happy to be there that, if duty permitted, I could almost wish to become a monk among them. He smiled. Then, fearing perhaps that I was in earnest, said they had quite enough already.'

During the next two days, while Napoleon's army was streaming into Moscow and the Russians were setting the whole city on fire, Serope helped Henry to prepare for his onward journey into Turkey. He had to abandon his trunks, his portable table, his chair, some of his books and sugar, and repack everything into bags. Melcom, a trusted servant of the monastery, well armed and Turkish speaking, was added to the party. 'The roads in Turkey being more infested with robbers than in Persia, a sword was brought for me.'

He had a last talk with Serope about his proposed reformation. 'He is bold and very able, but he is not spiritual. Perhaps that was the state of Luther at first. It is an interesting time in the world. All things proclaim the approach of the kingdom of God and Armenia is not forgotten.' On his part Serope was amazed to find this 'beardless youth, very delicate and thin', not only so learned but such an eminent Christian, in contrast to all other Englishmen he had met. Early on 17 September he escorted Henry and his party for an hour as they rode off westwards across the plain of Ararat.

When they reached the Araxes again, Melcom stayed back with Henry while he bathed. They rejoined the others at a village where the headman was reading the Koran with gun, sword and pistol by his side. 'He chanted the Arabic well and asked me if I knew that that book was nothing less than the great Koran.'

In view of the dangers of the road three more armed men joined them. But the only alarm was what they themselves caused a group of Armenians who were bringing firewood to their village on the high tableland where Russia, Persia and Turkey were all in sight together. At

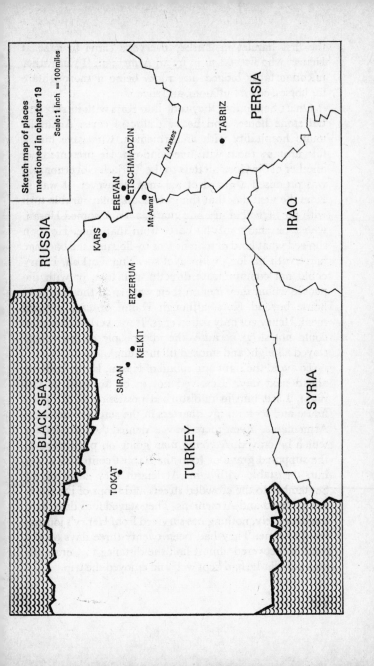

Sketch map of places
mentioned in chapter 19

Scale: 1 inch = 100 miles

the first hamlet in Turkey everyone came to gaze at Henry, who was taken in by an Armenian. 'I was rather uncomfortably lodged, my room being a thoroughfare for horses, cows, buffaloes, and sheep.'

On 21 September they rode into Kars with its substantial stone houses and heavy traffic of carts. Again he found hospitality with an Armenian, who gave him a fine upstairs room with five windows. He presented yet another of Sir Gore's letters to the Turkish Governor and was promised a guard of ten men. However, it was in Kars the next day that things took an unfavourable turn with the arrival of just one guard, a Turk named Hasan, who took charge of the party from that time. He soon showed what kind of man he was by flogging the baggage horse with his long whip. Not speaking Turkish, Henry could not communicate directly with him, or with the people whom they met on their way, so at the first post-house beyond Kars, although Hasan ordered a good meal, Henry got only rotten eggs. It was very cold and he could not sleep because 'the idle people of the village stayed all night and smoked till morning'.

To avoid the sight and sound of Hasan, Henry rode on ahead next day. 'Resolved not to be annoyed as last night, I left him in undisturbed possession of the post-house and took up my quarters in the stable-room at an Armenian's.' Even there he was denied the seclusion for which he craved. A young man going on pilgrimage to the supposed grave of John the Baptist contrived to get into the stable with him. At length they came on 25 September to the crowded streets and shops of Erzerum, full of Turks and Armenians. They stayed four days, but, unfortunately, nothing has survived from Henry's journal for that time. They had been twenty-three days on the road and covered almost half the distance to Constantinople. So far he had kept well and enjoyed the trip.

They left Erzerum at 2 p.m. on 29 September. 'We moved to a village where I was attacked with fever and ague.' It is not clear why this should have happened so soon after the four-day pause. 'I took nothing but tea next day and was rather better.' But on 1 October they were riding through the mountains for thirteen hours, and at night he was sick and faint. They heard that plague was raging at Tokat, which lay on their route. 'Thus I am passing inevitably into danger. O Lord, thy will be done. Living or dying, remember me.'

Next day Hasan set off at a great pace and made them all gallop much of the way to Kelkit, which they reached at sunset. 'At my request I was lodged in the stable of the post-house, not liking the scrutiny of the impudent fellows who frequent the coffee-room. As soon as it began to grow cold the ague came on and then the fever. In the night Hasan sent to summon me away, but I was quite unable to move. Finding me still in bed at dawn he began to storm furiously at my detaining him so long. He seemed determined to make up for the delay, for we flew over hill and dale to Siran, travelling all the rest of that day and all night. It rained most of the time. After sunset the ague came on again. In my wet state it was very trying and I hardly knew how to keep my life in me. There was a village at hand but Hasan knew no mercy. However, God being pleased to alleviate my sufferings, I went on contentedly till break of day.'

They reached some place about 100 miles east of Tokat, where Hasan was in danger of being arrested for having previously ridden a horse to death, so once more they hurried on till after dark. The thing which Henry feared had come upon him. He had fallen ill on the road in an unknown land, where he did not speak the language. He had no more letters of introduction and it was still 600 miles to Constantinople. Eventually 'I got off my horse, sat on the ground, and told him I neither could nor would go any further. He stormed but I was immovable. Then, seeing a light at a distance, I mounted and made towards it. I was taken to an open verandah, but Sergius told the people I wanted to be alone. This seemed very offensive to them. "Why must he be alone?" they asked, ascribing it to pride, I suppose. Tempted at last by money, they brought me to a stable-room. Hasan and others planted themselves there with me. My fever increased to a violent degree. The fire made me frantic. I entreated them to put it out or to carry me outside, but Sergius believed me delirious and was deaf to all I said. At last I pushed my head in among the luggage on to the damp ground and slept.'

When he rallied a little next day Hasan hurried him off again, though it proved only a short stage to the end of some pass where 'I was pretty well lodged at a poor little village in the jaws of the mountains. I was tolerably well till after sunset, when the ague came on with a violence I had never before experienced. I felt as if in a palsy, my teeth chattering and my whole frame shaking violently.' In this extremity two Persian travellers suddenly appeared and came at once to see if they could help him. 'They appeared quite brotherly after the Turks. While they pitied me, Hasan sat with perfect indifference ruminating on the further delay this was likely to cause. The cold fit was followed by a fever which lasted the whole night and prevented sleep.'

And so 6 October 1812 dawned without much hope for Henry; but 'no horses being available I had an unexpected repose. I sat in the orchard and thought with sweet comfort and peace of my God, in solitude my company, my friend and comforter. Oh, when shall time give place to eternity? When shall appear that new heaven and new earth wherein dwelleth righteousness? There shall in no wise enter into it anything that defileth: none of that wickedness which has made men worse than wild beasts, none of those corruptions which add still more to the miseries of mortality, shall be seen or heard of any more.'

Meanwhile those he loved in England had not forgotten him. On 14 October Simeon went up to London and unpacked at India House the portrait of Henry which had been painted in Calcutta. At first sight of how worn he had become 'I could not bear to look upon it but turned away, covering my face and in spite of every effort to the contrary crying aloud with anguish'. Bystanders presumed he must be Henry's father. They were not far wrong.

Four days later Napoleon started his retreat from Moscow. In the horrors of that winter campaign tens of thousands of men vanished for ever in the rivers and snow-bound plains of Russia, north of the Black Sea. South of the Black Sea, in the mountains of Turkey, one other man was missing too.

Shortly before Christmas Lydia had Henry's letter of 12 July, written soon after he reached Tabriz. It told her of the dangerous state of his health and of his intention to try to reach England. 'Darkness and distress of mind have followed this information. Sleep has fled from my eyes. A fearful looking for of trial and affliction, however this affair ends, possesses my mind.' She did not really expect him to get through, yet the possibility that he might succeed gave her no pleasure. After New Year she admitted, 'the state of my beloved friend occupies my mind less than I sometimes think is reconcilable with a true affection for him. The truth is, the concerns of my soul are more pressing.'

Simeon too received the letter Henry wrote him on 12 July and began to think about looking after him if he arrived. But on 10 February 1813 he heard from Isaac Morier, father of Sir Gore Ouseley's secretary, in

Constantinople. Morier informed him that an Armenian named Sergius had brought him Henry's journal and belongings, saying that he had died at Tokat on or about 16 October and been buried by the Armenians in their cemetery. The last entry in the journal was the paragraph written in the orchard at the village in the jaws of the mountains. Nothing more was ever found out about the last ten days of his life.

Simeon at once wrote to Calcutta to tell Thomason that 'our beloved brother has entered into the realms of glory and rested for ever in the bosom of his God'. Lydia had his letter on 14 February. 'I felt this afternoon as if he was present as I sat alone in the garden. I rejoice that no storms can molest those who die in the Lord. They rest from their labours of every kind. In heaven we shall meet and be united for ever.' It was more than seven years since she had seen him. She wished that she, or some friend, could have been with him at the end. Sometimes she felt he was near, consoling and protecting her, at other times a great sadness overwhelmed her, not least when in late April she had his last letter, written just before he started out from Tabriz.

When, in 1816, John Sargent published his *Memoir of the Rev. Henry Martyn*, it rapidly became a best-seller. Although the actual name of Lydia was suppressed in it, she was embarrassed to find her secret trumpeted throughout the land. She continued to live obscurely at Marazion with her mother, remembering annually the day of Henry's death with deep emotion. Ten years afterwards she put up his portrait under the cross on the wall of her room, which looked out over Mount's Bay where he had disappeared so long ago. But his death did not really make any great difference to her. Ever since 1800 she had lived with a lover gone away but affectionately remembered. First it was Samuel John in Penzance and London; then Henry in India; then Henry in heaven.

Posterity has tended to be hard on the girl who did not go, who missed the great chance and duty of her life by not accepting Henry's invitation to marry him in India. But to know all might be to forgive all. In the course of time she developed cancer and was ill for several years. She died unmarried in 1829 at the age of fifty-four.

Once he knew that Henry was with Christ, Simeon overcame his aversion to the portrait from Calcutta and for a quarter of a century it hung above the fireplace in his dining-room. 'There, see that blessed man,' he used to say. 'No-one looks at me as he does. He never takes his eyes off me. And he always seems to be saying, "Be serious, be in earnest. Don't trifle, don't trifle." And I won't trifle, I won't.' He bequeathed it to Cambridge University Library. It hung there for a hundred years and is on view in Cambridge to this day.

Henry had left the original manuscript of the Persian New Testament with the British Ambassador in Tabriz. When Sir Gore heard of his death he had several copies made and succeeded in presenting one of these to the Shah, as Henry himself had hoped to do. Sir Gore then took the original with him to Russia and, in 1815, a first edition was printed at St Petersburg by the Russian Bible Society. Sir Gore helped to correct the proofs. Meanwhile one of the copies which had been made in Shiraz reached Calcutta, and Seid Ali was invited to come and watch over the printing of the second edition which came out in 1816. He brought with him the original of Henry's translation of the Psalms, which was also published the same year. Other editions were brought out in London.

In 1846 Henry's New Testament and Psalms formed part of a magnificent complete Persian Bible printed in Edinburgh. Whereas previously only the four Gospels had been available, Henry's New Testament held the field for seventy years, going through nine editions in that time and profoundly influencing the Persian New Testament ever since.

The Arabic New Testament translated by Sabat under Henry's supervision was also printed in Calcutta in 1816, and twice reprinted a decade later. It has now been long superseded, but it was the first separate New Testament translation into Arabic for two hundred years. The real tragedy of the last five months of Henry's life, in which he accomplished little except to ride himself to death, was that he did not complete the third phase of his plan to translate an Indian New Testament in India, a Persian New Testament in Persia and an Arabic New Testament in Arabia.

Meanwhile, in 1814, the Mission Press in Serampore printed the Urdu New Testament, which Henry and Mirza Fitrut had translated. There were sixteen editions of it in the next thirty-three years. When the first complete Urdu Bible came out in Calcutta in 1843 it was largely Henry's work which shaped the New Testament, and the version in use today is clearly a descendant of his.

Quite apart from his contribution as a Christian linguist in Asia, Henry's example of missionary zeal and self-sacrifice for Christ's sake has had lasting influence in England. This was largely due to John Sargent, whose biography of him came out in London in the same year as Henry's Persian and Urdu New Testaments were published in Calcutta. The book went through ten editions in twenty years and made Henry famous. Throughout the nineteenth century his remarkable achievements and tragic death carried an irresistible appeal to Christians, stirring them up to proclaim the gospel all over the world. It was rumoured that the Armenians at Tokat had given him a funeral worthy of a patriarch of their ancient church. His end was likened to that of St Chrysostom, who was hounded to death in the same region so long before. His journal was compared to the *Confessions* of St Augustine, and Sally was likened to Monica.

Now that almost two centuries have passed, the story of Henry Martyn has not lost its significance. In a world at war he sought first the kingdom of God, risking his life in Christ's service and finding fulfilment in incessant toil. Although he himself never saw any of his translations printed, his work was not in vain, for he made the New Testament available in their mother tongue to tens of millions in India and Persia. Henry was one of the greatest linguists God ever gave his church. He stands with Carey at the beginning of the remarkable missionary service of Christians from the West, which followed the widespread evangelism of Wesley and others. Refusing to live for himself, he was glad to be spent out for his Saviour. He combined the convictions of an evangelical Christian, the mind of a brilliant scholar, and an almost monastic self-discipline. He was thirty-one years old when he died.

Sources for the biography of Henry Martyn

The following are the most important sources for the story of Henry Martyn.

1. John Sargent, *Memoir of the Rev. Henry Martyn B.D.* (Hatchard, London, 1816), 509 pp. There were many editions of this book, whose author was one of Henry's closest Cambridge friends. He based his account on Henry's journals and a narrative written by Henry himself of his life at Shiraz.

2. *Journal and Letters of the Rev. Henry Martyn B.D.*, in two volumes, edited by Samuel Wilberforce (Seeley and Burnside, London, 1837), 934 pp. Samuel Wilberforce, who later became Bishop of Oxford, was the son of William Wilberforce and the son-in-law of John Sargent. Published after Lydia's death, this book reveals more than was thought desirable when Sargent wrote. However, the reader is presumed to have Sargent's book in front of him. There are frequent cross-references to it, and quotations from Henry already given by Sargent are not repeated by Wilberforce (whose book is thus at times hardly intelligible without a knowledge of Sargent's). It consists exclusively of selections from Henry's journal and letters without any editorial comment or additional biographical information at all.

3. *The Diary of Lydia Grenfell*. This is preserved in the library of the Royal Institution of Cornwall at Truro. It covers the period from her twenty-seventh birthday on 19 October 1801, to 18 June 1826. A voluminous journal of some 2000 pages, it is strictly religious, confined almost entirely to her inward and spiritual feelings, rarely mentioning facts or events. Its highly subjective, introspective

character probably gives an unbalanced impression of Lydia, but here and there it contains priceless details about Henry and her relationship to him.

4. George Smith, *Henry Martyn, Saint and Scholar* (Religious Tract Society, London, 1892), 572 pp. This is the definitive biography. A great deal of valuable material is to be found only in this book, though in style and approach it is now as completely out of date as Sargent's.

5. Constance Padwick, *Henry Martyn, Confessor of the Faith* (Inter-Varsity Fellowship, London, 1953), 180 pp. This book, originally published by the Student Christian Movement in 1922, gave Henry a new lease of life for fifty years.

There have been a number of briefer biographies included in books of wider scope.

1. Marcus Loane, *Cambridge and the Evangelical Succession* (Lutterworth Press, London, 1952) contains a fifty-page account of Henry's life.

2. Marcus Loane, *They were Pilgrims* (Angus and Robertson, Sydney, 1970) includes a revised version of the same account.

3. Iain Murray (ed.), *Five Pioneer Missionaries* (Banner of Truth Trust, London, 1965) contains a sixty-eight-page article on Henry by Richard T. France.

Still shorter studies of Henry have been numerous.

G. C. B. Davies, *The Early Cornish Evangelicals 1735–60*, (SPCK, London, 1951), 221 pp., which is mainly a study of the Rev. Samuel Walker of Truro, gives an excellent picture of the social, economic and religious situation in western Cornwall during the youth of Henry Martyn's father.

Unfortunately the original journal, the most valuable source of all for a knowledge of Henry Martyn's life,

seems to have disappeared. Most of it was committed to
Corrie in India and sent by him to Henry's executors,
Charles Simeon and John Thornton, in 1814. The latter
part of the journal came into the hands of Isaac Morier
in Constantinople and was sent by him to Simeon and
Thornton in 1815. There was a prolonged reading of the
journal in Simeon's rooms at Cambridge about that
time. Sargent had it for his 1816 biography. Wilberforce
had it in 1837. But there the trail disappears.

Dr George Smith never alludes to the original journal
in his exhaustive work of 1892. All his quotations from
the journal are derived from Sargent and Wilberforce.
He could not go behind them and neither can we today.
Exhaustive enquiries have not yielded the slightest clue
to its whereabouts. It may have been destroyed after
the publication of Wilberforce's extracts. If it could be
found, a further biography of Henry would probably be
necessary. We could find out what he wrote in it in Latin
and Greek for eight months of 1809, none of which has
ever been revealed. We could learn what happened at
Erzerum during the last four days before the onset of his
final illness. We could mine what Sargent and Wilberforce, with their now distant viewpoints, did not think
worth mining. We would surely find we had struck gold.

In spite of the shortness of Henry's life and the disappear-
ance of his original journal, his biographers are all faced
with the task of summarizing many thousands of pages of
data by him and about him. So much that he wrote cries
out for quotation. At times I have felt it right to alter the
order of his words, to omit unnecessary ones, and occasionally to substitute a modern word for an outdated one
in order to preserve the crisp appeal of the original. In no
case have I tampered with his meaning. The one uniform
change I have made is to write 'Urdu' where he wrote
'Hindustani'.